Play it again, Slam

S0-BNX-825

Phillip and Robert King

B. T. Batsford Ltd, *London*

First published 1999

© Phillip and Robert King 1999

ISBN 0 7134 8299 0

A CIP catalogue record for this book is available from the British Library.

Typeset by KEATS, Harrow on the Hill

Printed by Creative Print and Design (Wales), Ebbw Vale, Wales
for the publishers,
B. T. Batsford Ltd, 583 Fulham Road,
London SW6 5BY

A BATSFORD BRIDGE BOOK
Series Editor: Tony Sowter

CONTENTS

INTRODUCTION

In one of the best-loved movies of all time, Rick, Ilse and Victor struggled valiantly to help save the world from the forces of evil. In the parody *Play it Again, Slam*, their motives are equally noble, but rather more modest, as they attempt to rescue the bridge world from the evils of a convoluted bidding system.

The Fall of Freddie Haversham is a pastiche of Somerset Maugham, in the days when playing bridge in casual wear was as unthinkable as eating peas with a knife.

Bridge of Spies is not a pastiche of anything in particular, but a warning of how an apparently respectable bridge club might become a front for an attempt to bring down civilisation as we know it.

Special thanks are due to Su Burn for her editing; any typographical errors are a consequence of the modest size of her fee. We are also grateful to Sue King, a not too distant relative, for the map which demonstrates the impossibility of escaping from Europe to America without passing through Casablanca.

William Somerset Maugham
1874-1965

Novelist, playwright, short story writer, qualified surgeon and bridge player.

When Willy Maugham's first novel appeared, he was hailed as the new Emil Zola. Inevitably, reviewers changed their minds when he made the artistic error of writing best-sellers; but he remained true to his conviction that 'art for art's sake makes no more sense than gin for gin's sake.'

He achieved world-wide fame when more than twenty of his works were successfully filmed. In several of them he actually appeared as a character (usually played by that distinguished actor, Herbert Marshall), commenting cynically on the follies of the other characters.

By this time, Maugham's critical reputation wasn't worth a wart on Virginia Woolf's toe. Then a miracle happened. As he approached the age of ninety, it was discovered that, through no fault of his own, he had become one of the Grand Old Men of English letters. It was recalled that he had even written a novel, *Cakes and Ale*, exposing the tendency of the English to make Grand Old Men out of octogenarian authors. Now he was more than a novelist; he was a prophet.

His critical reputation continues to wax as his mass appeal wanes. It is now fashionable to describe many of his stories as masterpieces. And quite right too.

1

THE FALL OF FREDDIE HAVERSHAM

I am not impressed by titles and I have no patience with those who set out to cultivate people of great birth. My acquaintance with a few dozen assorted lords and three or four dukes has persuaded me that intelligence is inversely proportional to rank. I mentioned this to King George recently and he was tickled to death when I assured him that he was an exception.

There was no need to inform Lady Veronica Chaverly that she was an exception. She knew. Nevertheless, I was mildly pleased when I spotted her in the Savoy, toying with a dry Martini while she planned her lunch.

"This is a bit of luck," I said. "Will you take pity on a lonely man and let me sit with you?"

"With pleasure," she smiled. "I hate to admit it, but I have been stood up."

"Really?" I hoped my tone conveyed that delicate blend of sympathy and surprise which such a catastrophe merited. I never knew Veronica when she was a girl, but when people told me she was lovely I could well believe it; for now, though nearly thirty, she was still ravishing.

As the daughter of a fourteenth duke, she had received the mandatory education in how to ride, dance, write cheques and sparkle at dinner parties.

It was not until contract bridge replaced auction that she discovered that she possessed an intellect.

She played quickly, boldly and with science. For a woman whose knowledge of literature was limited to the society magazines and Agatha Christie's lighter novels, her appetite for study seemed gargantuan. She had the theories of Sims and Vanderbilt at her elegant fingertips. She could recall every hand from all the big matches, and describe the players' errors with a delightfully acid wit. "The opening lead is the best part of Margot's defence," she once said of an eminent rival. "It is one of the few occasions when she is unlikely to revoke."

"I'm very grateful to whomsoever stood you up," I said, at the top of my grammatical form. "He must either be a cad or a fool. Unless he had a good excuse, like the simultaneous deaths of several close relatives."

I almost missed her reply. I was busy scribbling my *bon mot* on to the menu. It would fit nicely into my next two plays.

"It was Freddie Haversham," she sighed. "His Gold Cup match had been rearranged for this morning, and he couldn't find a substitute who could count up to thirteen without removing a sock."

"Now that is an excuse," I scribbled. "It makes a few relations popping off seem almost trivial."

"I knew you would understand." Her lovely blue eyes twinkled with amusement.

She had never married; such was her passion for bridge that she had resolved to wed no man who was not only handsome and well-bred, but able to match her brilliant play. While not in Veronica's class (dear Dick Lederer once classified me as a good player of the third rank), I knew enough to recognise the few who were. Only three possessed all the qualities she demanded.

One was an American whose descent from a Mayflower family seemed a passable substitute for breeding, until Veronica learned that the ancestor in question was a deck-hand.

The second was an Austrian nobleman with a detached castle in Saltzburg, but, after a brief visit, she decided that her contempt for his pedestrian bidding was equalled by her disdain for Mozart.

The other contender, and the current short-odds favourite, was Freddie Haversham.

"Perhaps Freddy's standing you up was a subtle avoidance play," I said. (By now the menu was crammed with wit, but there was still a tiny space between the *hors d'oeuvres* and the *poisson*.) "I can never pick up a bridge magazine without coming across one of his coups."

"I know." She smiled wryly. "It wouldn't surprise me if they named a miraculous squeeze after him."

"Is he really as good as they say?"

"I've no idea," she replied, rather coolly, I thought. "I'm told he plays the cards like a master, and bids like a schoolboy. But I've never seen him play."

"I must say I find that hard to believe."

"Must you? He only rose to the top a year or so ago, and since then ..." She gave a charming little shrug. "I suppose you might say I've been avoiding him."

"I wonder why?" I sensed that there was enough material here for three short stories, a play and a novel. Then, infuriatingly, she changed the subject by thrusting that morning's bridge problem in front of me, and I was left wondering.

"Have you read Major Bulstrode's latest piece of self-adulation?" she asked.

"Fortunately not," I shuddered.

I have always despised those authors who, when writing a bridge story, disturb the narrative drive with such extraneous matters as bridge. But as a writer of integrity, I have always placed truth above art. Veronica gave me a deal: I am honour bound to include it. Besides, as will become apparent, it was to have a profound effect on the lives of two people.

Realising that Veronica was longing to shine at my expense, I skimmed through the Bull's column with what I hoped was a bovine expression.

Bridge With Bulstrode

Love All. Dealer South.

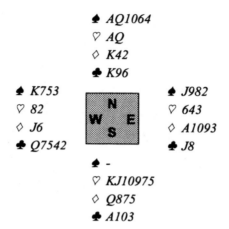

♠ AQ1064
♡ AQ
◊ K42
♣ K96

♠ K753   ♠ J982
♡ 82   ♡ 643
◊ J6   ◊ A1093
♣ Q7542   ♣ J8

♠ -
♡ KJ10975
◊ Q875
♣ A103

West	North	East	South
			1♡
Pass	1♠	Pass	2♡
Pass	3♣	Pass	3♡
Pass	6♡	All Pass	

Holding the East cards, I was forced to endure one of those interminable auctions which nowadays pass for bidding. Playing the Bulstrode System, the slam would be reached in two bids.

The four of clubs was led to my knave and declarer's ace. When she played a diamond to dummy's king, I won and correctly returned the suit. Now declarer, a promising player, successfully finessed the club nine, ruffed a spade, and had enough entries to set up the long spade for her twelfth trick.

My regular readers will easily see where West slipped up. He should have deprived declarer of a vital entry by inserting the queen of clubs on the second round of the suit.

"Not exactly the deal of the century," I said, ostentatiously stifling a yawn.

She gave me an arch look, which should have told me something, but didn't. "Then you agree with the Bull's analysis?"

"Of course," I said. "The idea of inserting an honour appears in most textbooks, usually on page twenty-five."

"True. What a pity the poor dear hadn't read page twenty-six. He should have blocked the suit by playing the eight of clubs on the first round." I was about to give a well-timed gasp of admiration, but there was more to come. "Failing that," she continued, "he could have saved his bacon when he came in with the ace of diamonds."

"How?" I asked her. It seemed the thing to do.

"By switching to a club, of course."

"So he could," I agreed in an awed whisper. "What a shame you can't expose the charlatan."

"Oh, but I shall. The deal will appear in next week's *Country Life*, pointing out East's lapses. And the Bull will have only himself to blame. Describing declarer as a promising player was unforgivably patronising."

"Why should that concern you?"

"I was declarer."

And now I can get back to the plot. We chose an amusing Chablis with our lobsters, and a memorable Chambertin with our pheasants. The soufflé was let down by a Chateau d'Yquem that had seen better days, but Veronica, always the soul of tact, said it reminded her of me. My Spartan diet forbade liqueurs after lunch, but I could never resist the fine old brandy which the maître d'hôtel always put by for me. I watched Veronica take a sip with evident satisfaction. This was surely the moment of truth, or at least a Bowdlerised version of it.

"Now you can tell me all about Freddie," I said.

"Oh, I don't want to talk about him." She tossed her exquisite head. "Freddie is too utterly...utterly."

Only the splendour of my cognac enabled me to endure the poverty of her language. I can forgive tautology, and have done so on several occasions, but "too utterly" was a painful reminder of the maddening success of our younger playwrights. Then, before I could pose my next penetrating question, we were interrupted by Henri, the sommelier with the peaches-and-cream complexion, the long eyelashes and the accent half-way between Toulouse and Liverpool. As he replenished my glass I gave him a nod of approval.

"Excellent," I smiled. "One should always hold a bottle by the neck and a woman by the waist."

"Preferably both at once," said Veronica, her fine eyes dancing with mischief.

"That will do, Henri." I left him to decide whether I referred to the brandy or the way he fluttered his eyelashes at Veronica. But I hope I am not a vindictive man. I resolved that he would have no cause to deprecate the size of my tip. There wouldn't be one.

"Where is the too utterly Freddie playing his match?" I enquired casually.

"At the Mayfair Club. It should be over by mid-afternoon. He told me he would be staying on afterwards. I said I might drop in for a rubber or two." She avoided my eyes. "Perhaps you would like to come with me?"

"The Clash of the Titans," I murmured. "I wouldn't miss it for words."

I waited for her to bare her soul, but she munched a *petit four* in comparative silence. I still had a trump card to play, and I played it. I lit a Havana and smiled enigmatically. I have learned from Sigmund Freud that women are jealous of cigars, and from experience that they are bewildered by enigma. Those twin menaces were bound to squeeze the truth out of her.

"Too utterly what?" I demanded, between smoke-rings.

To my immense horror, she smiled enigmatically. For one dreadful moment I thought she was going to light a cigar.

"It's a pity he has no title," I observed provocatively.

"He is descended from Edward the First." She was defiant, regal, snobbish.

"My dear Veronica," I was implacable, earthy, plebeian. "Genealogists assure me that fifty per-cent of the population have Plantagenet blood. I sincerely hope I belong to the other half."

"I'm sure that you have nothing to worry about," she smiled, and holding her adorable nose in the air, she swept off to powder it. As I settled down for a long wait, it dawned on me that Freud was decidedly overrated.

Veronica returned in slightly less than an hour, so we strolled into the Mayfair Club in time for afternoon tea. Freddie's opponents had conceded at half-time. He greeted me like a long-lost brother.

"I loved your new book," he said. "There isn't a living author who understands human nature as well as you do."

I hastily revised my opinion that he owed his popularity to his boyish charm. It was due to his sincerity and his literary taste. I almost forgot that I had not published a book for two years.

"What is so special about *dead* authors?" I asked slyly.

"Oh, I never speak ill of them," he laughed.

Freddie was six foot one, with broad shoulders and a slim waist. He had a beautifully sculptured face, with dark, intelligent eyes, and a smile that took your breath away. He was – there is no other way of putting it – too utterly utterly. He was a second son. His father, the baronet, had married for a mountain of money, and had the good grace to leave a hill or two to Freddie. "Promise me you'll spend it wisely," the old man whispered on his death-bed. The young man made the promise, and he kept it. He hunted in the hunting season. He shot in the shooting season. He philandered in the philandering season, which for Freddie was from January to December. He was at home in the great hotels of London, Paris and the Riviera, where he knew the first names of half the head waiters and all the chambermaids.

I could tell at a glance that he had fallen for Veronica like a row of nine-pins. As their eyes met, I felt that I would soon be witnessing not a rubber of bridge, but a sensuous mating ritual. I sat, pen in hand, ready to record their first words. Perhaps they would inspire a revival of the great romantic novel.

"Any good hands from your match?" Veronica asked.

"There was a diamond game which might amuse you," he replied. "I've written it down."

He took a sheet of paper from his notecase. Veronica studied it for all of ten seconds, then passed it to me, as though the task of making eleven tricks could safely be entrusted to a lesser mortal.

♠ AKQ2
♡ A654
◇ K109
♣ 93

♠ 4
♡ 8732
◇ AQJ432
♣ K6

West	North	East	South
			1◇
Pass	2♠	Pass	3◇
Pass	4◇	Pass	5◇
All Pass			

"I was declarer," Freddie informed us. "The knave of spades was led. How would you play it, Willie?"

Realising that my role in this enthralling drama was merely to feed the leading actors, I picked up my cue like a veteran stage butler. "I should draw trumps, throw my clubs on dummy's spades, and pray that hearts were three-two."

"But what if they were four-one?" asked Veronica, introducing an element of tragedy.

"Then I would cash winners at high speed and pray for a revoke."

"Oh, but you can do better than that," she said. "If trumps are two-two, you can give yourself an extra chance. Freddie found it."

"How on earth do you know that?" I remonstrated.

"If he hadn't, he'd never have shown us the deal. Confession may be good for the soul, but it's bad for one's reputation. Watch." She produced a gold pencil and began to tick off cards with indecent speed. "You cash three top spades, pitching clubs. Then a club ruff, a trump to dummy and another club ruff. Now a second trump to dummy and, if both opponents follow, you ruff the losing spade in hand."

She paused, to allow me to gaze, with a servile grin, at the five-card ending:

$$\spadesuit \ -$$
$$\heartsuit \ A654$$
$$\diamondsuit \ 9$$
$$\clubsuit \ -$$

$$\spadesuit \ -$$
$$\heartsuit \ 8732$$
$$\diamondsuit \ Q$$
$$\clubsuit \ -$$

"*Voilà!*" Veronica's monologue continued. "You play a heart towards dummy and, whatever West does, you duck. If either defender wins with a singleton honour, he will be forced to give you a ruff and discard." She turned confidently towards Freddie. "Is that how you played?"

"It's exactly how it went in the other room," he said. "And East happened to hold the bare queen of hearts. But our West was Claude Stukely."

"A useful defender," she nodded. "Of course he rose with the king, to swallow his partner's queen. One down. I suppose it was a game swing?"

"Well," said Freddie, "I'm afraid my left hand opponent was a bit of a tiger, quite capable of emulating Claude's crocodile coup. So after the opening lead I was pondering sagely, when the waiter arrived with a half bottle of champagne I had ordered earlier. By the time it had been opened, tasted and poured, East, who was the irascible Humphrey Glossop, signalled his impatience and his suit length by banging the seven spades on the table, before I had played from dummy."

He paused, as if to allow the significance of this to sink in. In my case it floated serenely on the surface, but Veronica saw the point immediately.

"What a stroke of luck!" she exclaimed. "Knowing that the spades were almost certainly four-four, you could combine two chances – finding the hearts three-two, or the king of clubs onside." She eyed him critically. "You ducked the spade, of course?"

"I did indeed."

"Very pretty. It deserves to appear in tomorrow's *Times*."

"I'm told it will. Anyway, it didn't matter what West did at trick two, but he glared balefully at Humphrey, and switched to a trump. I took in dummy and rattled off my three top spades..."

"... discarding three losing hearts. Then you cashed the heart ace, ruffed a heart..."

"... and when they broke four-one, I simply drew another round of trumps, and played a club towards the king. And at last luck was with me." He paused, to savour Veronica's approval. She didn't exactly do a valedictory handstand, but her faint smile seemed to satisfy him as he showed us the full deal:

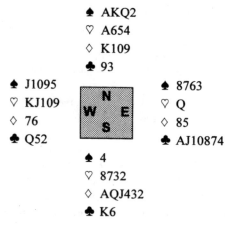

```
                    ♠ AKQ2
                    ♡ A654
                    ◇ K109
                    ♣ 93
    ♠ J1095                        ♠ 8763
    ♡ KJ109        N               ♡ Q
    ◇ 76        W     E             ◇ 85
    ♣ Q52          S               ♣ AJ10874
                    ♠ 4
                    ♡ 8732
                    ◇ AQJ432
                    ♣ K6
```

"You did well," I said. Somebody had to say it, I thought.

"Not as well as Veronica." He shook his head. "She spotted the right line more quickly than I did."

"It's always harder at the table," she said. "How did the Glossop take it?"

"He berated me for dawdling over a contract he would have made without drawing breath. He said that if I was going to rely on finding the club king onside, I should have tackled the suit immediately after drawing trumps."

"Poor fellow," she said. "Was it late in the match?"

"Almost the last board."

"That explains it. His brain cell must have been tired."

I was about to make a significant contribution to the dialogue when we were informed that a table was up.

Veronica drew Mrs Belvedere, a pleasant widow of eighty summers, and an even larger number of winters. Yet she retained all her faculties; it was unfortunate that none of them enabled her to play bridge.

A noted wit once wrote (I have forgotten in which of my stories it appeared) that there were two classes of partner. One was so bad that you lost all your money. The other was so good that you lost all your confidence. I settled back to watch the two ladies prove my theory.

"I prefer a very simple system, my dear," Mrs Belvedere ventured timidly.

"How wise of you, Mrs Belvedere." Veronica's smile was feline, as she shuffled the cards with blinding speed. "We'll play by the book, Culbertson's for preference."

"And a strong no trump if you don't mind."

"Absolutely, partner. You should have at least six honour tricks," Veronica agreed. "However, I shall open on three."

"And Blackwood?" Mrs Belvedere pleaded.

"Very well, but not for part-scores, please."

Freddie had cut the intrepid General Trumpington, and he gave him a boyish grin. "I don't know about you, partner," he said, "but I play by the light of nature."

"So do I, my boy," the General said. "Can't abide all these newfangled gadgets. The forcing two clubs is my limit, and it comes up so seldom, I always forget it."

"Then I shall do the same, Sir." Freddie laughed appreciatively. "Signals?"

"Don't you worry about 'em. Just watch my face and you'll know exactly what I've got."

"Message received and understood, General." Freddie gave him a witty little salute. "I think I'm going to enjoy this rubber."

It struck me that Freddie was almost good enough to eat, but I contented my self with a buttered crumpet.

Love All. Dealer East.

Mrs Belvedere
- ♠ 4
- ♡ AK973
- ◊ K6
- ♣ AQ954

Freddie
- ♠ 9872
- ♡ 1054
- ◊ 73
- ♣ 10862

```
      N
   W     E
      S
```

General Trumpington
- ♠ K6
- ♡ QJ62
- ◊ AQ52
- ♣ KJ3

Veronica
- ♠ AQJ1053
- ♡ 8
- ◊ J10984
- ♣ 7

West	North	East	South
		1NT	2♠
Pass	3NT	Dble	4♠
Pass	Pass	Dble	All Pass

The General's doubles may seem a trifle forward, but he was a man who considered the Charge of the Light Brigade a little on the cautious side. When Mrs Belvedere bid no trumps first, it was not an act of mutiny; she had forgotten the system. Veronica's smile was forgiving as she converted to four spades, but I had never seen her look so tense as Freddie considered his opening lead.

He led a diamond. The General cashed two tricks and tried a third round of the suit. Sitting on Veronica's left, I could easily see how the play would go. West would ruff high in front of dummy. Later, declarer would be home and dry when she picked up the king of spades.

But, to my astonishment, Freddie ruffed with the spade deuce. This struck me as a beginner's error. Worse, it might well have spelled the end of his chances with Veronica. Without hesitation she over-ruffed on the table. It was only then that I appreciated Freddie's strategy, for now, when General Trumpington won the second round of trumps, he was able to give his partner another diamond ruff.

"By George!" he said. "When you played your two of spades, I was afraid you'd sunk us."

"I wasn't all that optimistic myself," said Freddie. "But to set the contract I needed to find you with the ace of trumps, in which case they would be down anyway." He smiled modestly. "Or the king doubleton, in which event I had to prevent declarer from taking the finesse."

"So you did, by Jove!" The General had a vocabulary of nearly a thousand words, and he had mastered every one of them.

"I was surprised when my four of spades took a trick," said Mrs Belvedere. "But would three no trumps have made?"

With Veronica as her partner, this was dicing with death, but Freddie made a life-saving intervention.

"As a matter of fact it would, as the cards lay," he said, "but your partner was quite right to take out to four spades."

"Which turned out to be unmakeable," said Veronica.

"Ah!" said Freddie.

"What do you mean by 'ah!'?" she asked.

"Nothing."

"Long speeches often mean nothing," she said. "Monosyllables are usually significant."

This was so clever, and so manifestly untrue, that I immediately made a note of it. On the stage it would pass as an epigram.

"Well," said Freddie, "I'm sure that in your position I would never have found the play, but you might have let my two of spades hold the trick."

I had never seen Veronica look so stunned, but she was a good enough player to see that he was right. Freddie's deuce would have been the defence's third and last trick. There was a steely glint in her eye as she dealt the cards, and I was sure he had soared in her estimation.

"It is a relief to discover that you're not perfect, Veronica," I said. "Men always pass a perfect woman with a respectful bow, when they are on their way to call on the other kind."

"By the way, General," said Freddie, breaking the stony silence which followed my quip, "I should never have thought of that defence but for your very astute double."

This was sheer moonshine, but Freddie's skill at buttering up partners was worth two hundred points a rubber.

He was also rather good with authors.

The next two deals were dull. Mrs Belvedere, with only thirteen top tricks, managed to scrape home in a heart game. The General drew level with a straightforward three no-trumps.

Then, just as I was completing an unforgettable aphorism on the human condition, Freddie drove it out of my mind with a piece of deception which, for an unmarried bachelor, was truly remarkable. Since Veronica was the victim, it is presented from her disadvantage point.

Game All. Dealer South.

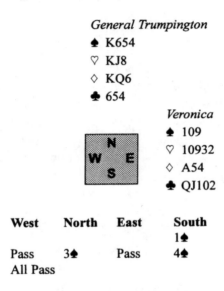

General Trumpington
♠ K654
♡ KJ8
◇ KQ6
♣ 654

Veronica
♠ 109
♡ 10932
◇ A54
♣ QJ102

West	North	East	South
			1♠
Pass	3♠	Pass	4♠
All Pass			

After Mrs Belvedere led the knave of diamonds, Freddie gave the matter a few seconds consideration before playing low from dummy. Veronica's analysis was even quicker. Freddie almost certainly had a singleton diamond, but was worried about a possible club switch through his weakness. It was obvious that his plan was to keep Mrs Belvedere on play until it was too late to switch, and Veronica was determined to upset it. Freddie probably held something like:

♠ AQJ83
♡ AQ64
◇ 4
♣ K83

If she played low, Freddie would be able to set up a tenth trick in diamonds at his leisure, leaving the defence powerless. Therefore, she confidently overtook her partner's knave with the diamond ace and fired back the queen of clubs. She even smiled when Freddie's king lost to the ace and the suit was continued. Unaccountably, Freddie ruffed the third club and claimed his contract. The full deal, much to Veronica's consternation, was:

General Trumpington
♠ K654
♡ KJ8
◇ KQ6
♣ 654

Mrs Belvedere   *Veronica*
♠ 72   ♠ 109
♡ 754   ♡ 10932
◇ J1098   ◇ A54
♣ A973   ♣ QJ102

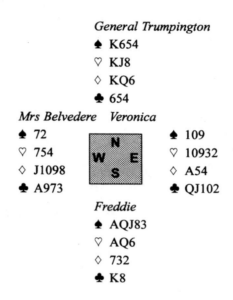

Freddie
♠ AQJ83
♡ AQ6
◇ 732
♣ K8

"Yes," she sighed. "A competent deceptive play."

I would have chosen a more fulsome epithet. It appeared that, among players of the first rank, "competent" was high praise.

"Thank you, Veronica," said Freddie.

"You realise that Mrs Belvedere might have led from a jack doubleton?"

"She might have," he agreed cheerfully.

"Suppose that in addition to five diamonds, I held the ace of clubs," she persisted. "Wouldn't you have botched a contract which with normal play was cold?"

I have always felt that the Socratic method should have died with Socrates, but Freddie took it well.

"Veronica," he smiled, "the contract was in perfectly safe hands – yours. Rising with the ace of diamonds was a master play, and I would have staked my life on your finding it."

"How courageous of you," she said, while I wondered why his compliment gave her so little pleasure.

"Never mind, Veronica," I commiserated. "Remember Molière's doctors. Your defence, like their operations, was performed with style. The death of the patient was incidental."

The look she gave me suggested that Molière was not her favourite playwright. Next time I would try Racine.

"A most enjoyable rubber," said the General. "Sorry I can't stay for another." He beamed at Freddie. "You and Lady Veronica should team up. I'd wager sovereigns to pesetas you'd win everything in sight."

Freddie was as pleased as a puppy with two tails. Veronica's expression was like a Henry James novel – completely unreadable. Surely she could recognise a perfect partner when she saw one.

After the General's tactical withdrawal, there was nobody free to fill the breach, and I was persuaded, much against my better judgement, to make up the table. I am by nature an onlooker, a professional observer, a cynical commentator on the frailties of others. Now I ran the considerable risk of revealing my own, and when Veronica and I drew the two highest cards, the risk became a certainty.

In my short story, *Sanatorium*, one of the inmates made a redoubled grand slam. Rather than describing the hand, I chose an amusing alternative: in his moment of triumph, the declarer died of a cardiac arrest. Praying for a similar diversion, I looked hopefully at the other three players, but they seemed distressingly healthy.

Desperate for some Dutch courage, I called for a strong champagne cocktail. By the time Veronica had finished instructing me in her system, I was halfway through my second.

I managed to deal the cards without mishap. (Veronica had always maintained that dealing was the best part of my game).

"And please remember," she instructed me, as I sorted my cards, "I don't mind you overbidding, but only when you are raising my suit."

"Of course," I responded tartly. "And would it be alright if I let you bid no trumps first?"

Love All. Dealer East.

Mrs Belvedere

♠ 54
♡ K104
◇ A7654
♣ AJ5

Veronica

♠ 87
♡ Q7652
◇ Q83
♣ Q94

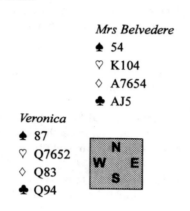

West	North	East	South
		Pass	1♠
Pass	2◇	Pass	4♠
Pass	4NT	Pass	5♡
Pass	6♣	All Pass	

My more perceptive readers may notice that once again I have presented the deal as a defensive problem. Veronica led the five of hearts, and Mrs Belvedere, who had not overbid her hand since the siege of Mafeking, laid out her dummy with a sheepish air.

"I'm afraid I may have been a little too daring," she said. "But you play the dummy so well."

"Flattery will get you everywhere, partner." Freddie smiled. "And you have all you promised, perhaps a little more."

He glanced briefly at Veronica's heart five, and called for the four. Impassively, I contributed the eight, and managed to conceal my surprise when he won with the ace. He drew trumps in three rounds, crossed to dummy's ace of diamonds and ruffed a diamond. Then, without a care in the world, he advanced the three of hearts.

Confident that a woman's guess is better than a man's certainty, Veronica, placing declarer with ♡AJ3, decided to rob him of an entry to the table by going in with the queen. Her expression when my heart knave landed on dummy's king beggared description, for these were the four hands.

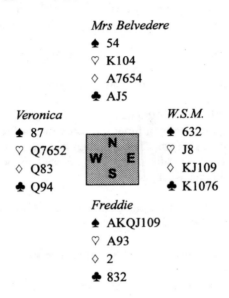

Mrs Belvedere
♠ 54
♡ K104
◇ A7654
♣ AJ5

Veronica
♠ 87
♡ Q7652
◇ Q83
♣ Q94

W.S.M.
♠ 632
♡ J8
◇ KJ109
♣ K1076

Freddie
♠ AKQJ109
♡ A93
◇ 2
♣ 832

I trust that the quality of my play is now apparent. I only wish Dick Lederer had been there to see it; he would have upgraded me on the spot. When playing my eight of hearts on the opening lead, I had experienced a warm glow, which was not entirely due to the champagne cocktails. The deal bore a striking resemblance to Major Bulstrode's thought for the day (elementary to a good player of the *second* rank.) Thanks to my defence, Freddie needed not only four entries to dummy to establish his long diamond, but a miracle in the heart suit, and clever little Veronica had provided one. Yet, seeing her icy stare, I felt like a convicted heretic, quaking before the Grand Inquisitor, and uncomfortably aware of a strong smell of paraffin.

"Did you really expect me to place you with the jack of hearts?" she cried.

"I can only pray for absolution," I said. "I had formed the impression that you were blessed with papal infallibility."

Freddie came gallantly to my rescue. "With deep respect, Veronica, the eight of hearts was a fine shot. And you were equally correct to insert your queen," he added hastily.

"I agree," I said, with malicious satisfaction. "Competently defended, partner." I purred expertly, and paused to savour the moment. "I'm afraid you were taken in by Freddie's masterly play of the heart ace at trick one."

"Really?" She smiled radiantly. "I thought he pulled the wrong card."

"You've seen through me." Freddie chuckled. "How did you guess?"

The rest was anti-climax. On the next deal, I brought home a four spades contract which required nothing more advanced than a Vienna Coup to set up a childishly simple squeeze. Then Veronica won the rubber with a routine no-trump game. Even Freddie could find no way to praise her, but he accepted defeat with his usual good grace.

"My fault, partner," he told Mrs Belvedere. "I had a cheap club sacrifice, but I'm afraid my nerve failed me."

"I'll forgive you," she giggled girlishly, "just this once."

I have always maintained that, although God may have created the World, it is the Devil who makes it go round, and I turned to Veronica with a Mephistophelian smile.

"I agree with the General," I said. "You and Freddie should form a regular partnership."

"Quite." She rose to leave, and smiled at Freddie with everything except her eyes. "I'll give you a ring after Christmas."

For some reason this seemed to give Freddie little satisfaction, but I suppose it was an odd thing to say in the middle of February. As we left, he looked like a man who had just been given a death sentence.

It was the least I could do to see Veronica home to Belgravia. Besides, I needed an ending for my story.

"Well," I said, "it seems that unless you acquire a taste for Mozart, or for the descendants of common deck-hands, you are fated to remain a spinster of this parish."

"I don't care," she said. "I realise now that I never really liked him."

"I don't understand you," I said. "Weren't you looking for an equal?"

"Yes," she almost screamed. "But not that bloody equal!"

I laughed. I laughed uncontrollably. The tears flowed onto my heaving chest. She was priceless, she was baffling, she was a woman.

"There is nothing sadder," she said, "than to spend your life searching for something, and then, when you've found it, to realise that it isn't what you wanted." She smiled bravely. "Who wrote that?"

"I shall," I replied promptly. "After some much-needed polish, it will appear in my next book."

"And what book is that?"

I thought for a moment. "I shall call it *The Fall of Freddie Haversham*," I announced.

She turned on me with a look of such tigerish ferocity that, though I blush to confess it, I quailed.

"If you dare put me in one of your cheap stories, I shall sue you," she cried. "After I've scratched your eyes out."

Suddenly, I remembered a remark dear John Barrymore once made to me. "Willy," he said, "there is only one way to fight a woman – with your hat. Grab it and run."

It seemed excellent advice. I took it.

Tribute to Casablanca

Once in a decade or so a work of popular entertainment fulfils its commercial objectives and then goes on to achieve far more than its creators intended.

Based on a play *Everyone Comes to Rick's*, Casablanca was a studio-bound Hollywood drama which, after a series of uncertainties, happy accidents, and the frenzied efforts of a dozen contributors to complete the screenplay a few hours before the final shot, fell together miraculously into an enduring cinematic masterpiece.

Or was it just a schlocky melodramatic B picture made bearable only by a great cast and a group of brilliant technicians?

Directed by Michael Curtiz, it starred Humphrey Bogart, Ingrid Bergman, Paul Henreid, Claude Rains, Conrad Veidt, Sidney Greenstreet, Peter Lorre, S Z Sakall and Doolie Wilson (who played most of the characters who turn up in the following parody). The superb script was by Julius Epstein, Philip Epstein and Howard Koch.

The idea of Casablanca (the town) being part of the escape route from occupied Europe is absurd, an invention to provide a romantic background for a four-handkerchief tear-jerker. And this was not the only example of not allowing historical accuracy to stand in the way of pure entertainment.

As the creators of Casablanca (the film) took so many liberties with history, the authors of *Play It Again, Slam* decided to take liberties with the liberties. We hope that fellow devotees of America's favourite film will not regard this as an act of sacrilege.

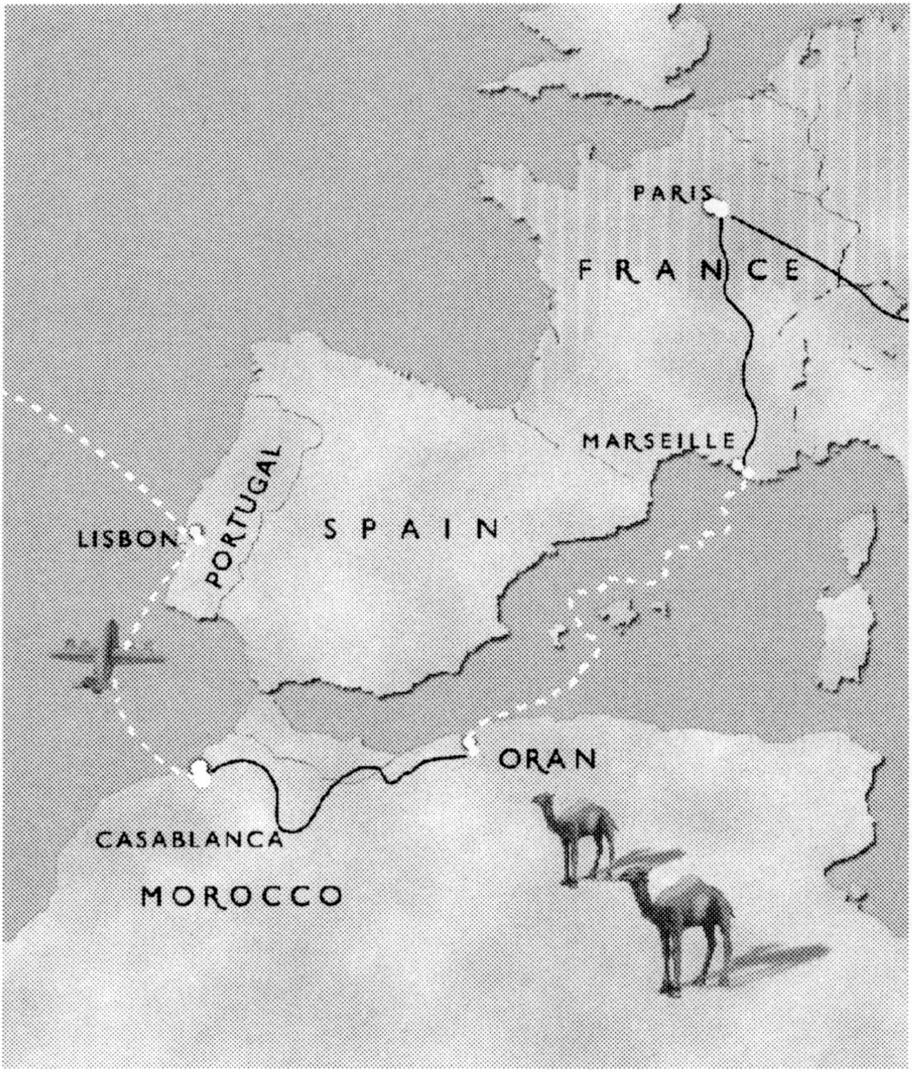
PARIS
FRANCE
MARSEILLE
LISBON
PORTUGAL
SPAIN
ORAN
CASABLANCA
MOROCCO

2
PLAY IT AGAIN, SLAM

PROLOGUE

It was nearly half-time in the Second World War, and the bad guys were well ahead. Groaning under the Nazi yoke, the people of occupied Europe began to gaze wistfully towards the Americas.

Soon, a roundabout refugee route sprang up. North-west to Paris, and due south to Marseilles; across the Mediterranean to Oran; then, by auto, camel, or on weary, blistered feet, due west along the sun-baked rim of Africa to Casablanca, in Free French Morocco. There, those with money, friends in low places, or the looks of Hedy Lamarr, obtained exit visas to take them north again, to Lisbon, the great embarkation point to the New World.

The unlucky ones remained in Casablanca, washing dishes in cafés and bars. Some of them were forced to become waiters. And wait, and wait ... and wait.

Many spent the long, lonely nights pondering the maddening riddle of why the escape route from Eastern Europe was so torturous. Little did they realise that, had it been more direct, the unthinkable would have happened; the greatest movie of all time would have been called "Rotterdam".

Chapter One

Captain Louis Delage watched Major Strafe arrange his cards with Teutonic precision. Spades to the left, followed by the other suits in strict order of rank; each suit in exact order of denomination. And, throughout, the German sat rigidly to attention, oblivious to the stifling heat. Strafe was the finished article: Nietsche's Superman had been a mere prototype.

"Forgive a poor, corrupt chief of police, Major." Louis was a life master of veiled insolence. "But the way you sort your hand is very revealing. An opponent less scrupulous than myself might take advantage."

"Only once, Captain Delage. After his first offence I would have him shot."

Louis was tempted to enquire the penalty for a second offence, but a glance at the stern face suggested that laughing at Gallic humour was not among the German's favourite pastimes.

The major opened one club. It wasn't his turn to bid, and he knew it. "I am sorry," he lied brazenly. "I have just recollected that you were the dealer."

"Was I?" Louis arched his eyebrows in mock astonishment. "Then I shall open one spade. Naturally, I shall waive the penalty."

"Naturally," Strafe sneered, mopping a bead of perspiration from his brow.

Louis revelled in his opponent's first sign of weakness. "You have my sympathy," he said. "The Blue Parakeet must seem like an oven to one who has so recently arrived from Berlin in midwinter."

"Not at all." The major was determined to prove he hadn't won the Iron Cross, third class, for nothing. "We Germans must get used to all climates, from the Sahara to Siberia."

The notion of Strafe in Siberia appealed to Louis. He wondered what such an important officer was doing in Casablanca, and why he had insisted on a bridge game so soon after his plane had landed.

Strafe's fat little number two, Herr Heinz, passed Louis' spade opening with fifty-two varieties of reluctance. Lieutenant Castel raised his chief to two spades and Strafe leapt straight to five clubs. "After my original error, I feel obliged to show my suit," he said, daring Louis to question his ethics.

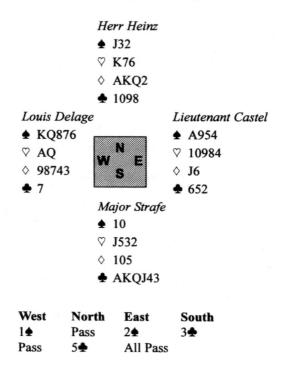

Herr Heinz
♠ J32
♡ K76
◇ AKQ2
♣ 1098

Louis Delage
♠ KQ876
♡ AQ
◇ 98743
♣ 7

Lieutenant Castel
♠ A954
♡ 10984
◇ J6
♣ 652

Major Strafe
♠ 10
♡ J532
◇ 105
♣ AKQJ43

West	North	East	South
1♠	Pass	2♠	3♣
Pass	5♣	All Pass	

Louis led the ♠K, noting the fall of his partner's nine and declarer's ten. After a rapid glance at dummy, he decided that the defensive prospects weren't worth a bent sou. To justify his bids Strafe needed a solid six-card trump suit and at least four hearts to the knave.

Repressing a shudder, he tried to imagine himself in the Nazi's jackboots. Not knowing about the remarkably lucky heart distribution, the Major would be praying for a defensive error. So Louis would fake one. All he needed was to find his partner with the ◇J, and declarer with the ◇10. Assuming the air of a hotheaded Gascon leading recklessly from an honour, he led the ◇3.

Strafe, who until that moment wouldn't have given a bent pfennig for his chances, brightened visibly. Humming the triumphant sword motif from *Siegfried*, he played low from the table, and stifled a Wagnerian oath when Castel's knave appeared. Winning the heart return, Louis couldn't resist whistling a few bars of the funeral march from *Götterdämmerung*.

"Our third trick, I'm afraid," he apologised.

Strafe gave him a look as black as a coal miner's bathwater. "You say that as if you expected there to be others," he complained.

"I am content with one down, Major. We French are always magnanimous in victory."

"Most commendable, particularly as you get so little practice." Strafe arrogantly examined his opponent's remaining cards. "So you had ace-queen doubleton heart! But for your bizarre diamond switch, I was fated to make my contract." He regarded the police chief through narrowed eyes. "Tell me, was your play an example of what you French call *panache*?"

"It was an example of what we French call bridge."

"Do I detect a note of criticism, Captain?"

"Heaven forbid, Major!" Louis laughed easily. "And even if there was, would you expect me to admit it?"

"My dear Captain, you forget my Gestapo training." Strafe laughed jovially, but it didn't fool Louis. "We have ways of making you talk."

"My dear Major, you forget that Casablanca is part of Free France."

"Free France is like a free lunch: there is no such thing."

"Oh dear! Does that mean you will have me shot?"

"Not necessarily." Strafe gave the Frenchman a humanitarian beam. "You have just lost a war; I cannot blame you for trying to win a little battle of words. But you are merely an official of the Vichy government, controlling that part of France which we have agreed not to occupy – for the time being."

"I take you point, Major. Freedom is a precious commodity. I suppose that is why you Germans ration it so strictly."

"Precisely. And now that you have shown yourself to be a competent bridge player, I should like to have a word with you. Alone."

The two junior officers withdrew obediently, and Strafe eyed Louis like a king cobra contemplating his lunch. "Captain," he seemed to hiss, "have you noticed anything unusual about the latest batch of refugees?"

"I don't think so. A few of them have the delightful odour of Camel Number Five, but that is nothing new."

"Then it must have escaped your notice that an astonishingly high percentage are expert bridge players."

This was news to Louis, but he was too vain to show it. "So we can look forward to some high level games," he said.

"Evidently." Strafe snapped his fingers. A magnum of champagne and a jar of caviar arrived miraculously. "German efficiency," he said, and raised his glass. "To the New Order."

Seduced by the Dom Perignon label, Louis echoed the toast. "The New Order," he said. "How is it going, by the way?"

"We are making progress. Soon everyone will think only what we allow them to think."

"A remarkable achievement."

"But inevitable. Once you have grabbed the people by the genitals, their hearts and minds will follow. Already they are reading only what we allow them to read."

"Book burning tends to have that effect," Louis remarked helpfully.

"Exactly." Strafe was delighted to have found an ally. "Art is well under control. So far we have destroyed half of those abstract monstrosities of which your countrymen are so fond."

"And Reichsmarschall Goering has abstracted the other half," Louis muttered.

"Pardon, Captain?"

"Nothing, Major. Please continue,"

"Music is not so easy to censor. However, we can safely say that Wagner is in, Mendelssohn is out, and that Schubert is reduced to the ranks."

"I'm pleased to hear it, Major. I've never forgiven him for not finishing that symphony."

"And we have never forgiven him for starting it."

"Very droll, Major. I was afraid that repartee had gone the way of Mendelssohn. And do those hordes of fleeing experts mean that bridge has gone the way of abstract monstrosities?"

"Hardly. The Third Reich are the reigning World Champions."

Louis stifled his protest as he remembered that Austria was now part of the burgeoning Third Reich.

"Never underrate the propaganda value of games," said Strafe, placing a large scoop of caviar onto a minute piece of toast. "Think of the prestige those Russian barbarians have gained from chess."

"And from caviar," said Louis, swallowing a modest mouthful. "But if your bridge stars are such heroes, why are they deserting in such grotesque numbers?"

Strafe stiffened. "They are traitors," he declared. "They refuse to adopt the great German bidding system."

Louis wondered whether that included out-of-turn bids and shamelessly informative passes. Strafe seemed to read his thoughts.

"Forget the crude methods I am forced to employ with that fool Heinz," he said. "Our system is a masterpiece of logic, honed to perfection by the finest mathematicians in Germany. It is based on an artificial club opening, reinforced by seventy-nine conventions and the number is increasing daily. Its flawless precision has never been approached by the decadent democracies." He gazed fanatically into the distance, as if striving to recall the words of Doktor Goebbels' latest bridge bulletin. "It is the apotheosis of Prussian discipline."

"Pardon me, Major. You have used a word I do not understand."

"Apotheosis?"

"Discipline."

"Very droll, Captain. I am glad that kindergarten humour hasn't gone the way of the French army. Let me tell you that after five rounds of disciplined bidding, we can tell every card our partner holds." He smiled; not a pleasant sight. "And that he has an uncle with a frankfurter stand in Hamburg."

Louis manufactured an awe-struck whistle. "Incredible. But what if he has an uncle with a hamburger stand in Frankfurt?"

"I am sure we are working on it."

"Quite, Major. Already I detect a strong Viennese influence. Is it based on the work of Doctor Paul Stern?"

"Do not mention that upstart! He is an impostor, a mountebank."

"And a trifle Jewish, I believe. Say no more, Major. Who was the inventor?"

"Professor Ludwig von Erheim. His earliest published work pre-dates Stern's first scribblings by nearly a year."

"How convenient for you. I hope the ink is dry."

"I advise you to guard that tongue of yours, Captain. You would look rather silly without it. Now to business; the bridge refugees are not our main problem, they are a symptom. Yesterday two German agents were found shot. What steps are you taking?"

Louis fell back on his usual bromide. "We are rounding up twice the usual number of suspects."

"That is not enough."

"It is half the population of Casablanca. Nearly everyone in Casablanca is a shady character, which creates a vast number of suspects."

"Then I will give you a clue. The killer was undoubtedly the man they were tracking. He possesses papers which, if they fell into the wrong hands, could destroy our plans to dominate bridge. We believe he intends to sell them to an enemy of the Reich who is on his way to Casablanca. We must have those papers. The killer is an accomplished criminal, and probably a bridge expert."

"Then I promise you we will catch him tonight. He will be at Brick's. Everyone comes to Brick's."

Chapter Two

Everyone came to Brick's. It was a place where they could enjoy Hemingway without having to read him. They were hooked on the smell of sin and danger. They loved beating a path through the pickpockets and ring-pedlars to the place where Slam the piano-player pounded out songs from the days when life was sweet and clean. And incredibly boring.

Brick Lane leaned against the bar with a whisky sour and a grin to match, and eyed them as if humanity wasn't his favourite race. He wasn't very tall, and he wasn't very broad, but there was a look on his world-weary face which told you that if you stood in his way he'd slap you down and make you like it.

Nobody stood in his way as he finished his drink and started on his evening tour of the gambling rooms. He watched Emile the croupier spin his roulette wheel like a spider spinning its web. Emile made sure that the Germans lost heavily, and Captain Delage won steadily, and the house made a profit that stretched the laws of probability just short of the point where someone might notice.

Brick stayed for a while to admire Emile's illicit artistry. Then he strolled into the card room to see the high-stake bridge game. The kibitzers were perched around Ukarde, who was on a winning streak as long as an undertaker's face. Ukarde was a short, dapper man, with ingratiating ways and the endearing features of a good-looking gargoyle. He was Casablanca's shrewdest grifter and sharpest card player. Brick might have given him a run for his money, but Brick had not touched a card in anger since the day he left Paris, with his life in shreds and a million-dollar chip on his shoulder.

There was not an empty seat near Ukarde, so Brick looked around for someone to evict. He made his choice, and his hand landed heavily on the shoulder of the director of the Deutsche Bank.

"You've been barred," he said.

"Barred? For what reason?"

"Overbidding and underplaying."

"That is ridiculous! I am one of the finest players in Germany."

"This isn't Germany. So leave quietly and there'll be no trouble. Your cash is good in the john."

"This is an outrage! Do you know who I am?"

"I do. You're lucky the john's open to you."

The banker was marched off, threatening reprisals, and Brick settled down to watch the action.

Game All. Dealer North.

Bugatti
- ♠ 86
- ♡ AJ6
- ◇ AJ10985
- ♣ Q6

Diamond Merchant
- ♠ AJ1075
- ♡ KQ854
- ◇ 4
- ♣ 32

Palooka
- ♠ 32
- ♡ 92
- ◇ KQ76
- ♣ 109875

Ukarde
- ♠ KQ94
- ♡ 1073
- ◇ 32
- ♣ AKJ4

West	North	East	South
1♠	2◇	Pass	3NT
Pass	Pass	Dble	All Pass

The diamond merchant saw no percentage in honouring his partner's double by leading his lone diamond. He chose a deceptive ♡4, which ran to declarer's ten. Brick amused himself by figuring the deal from Ukarde's standpoint. With fifteen points missing, there was only one possible layout; West had opened light, with length in both majors, and East held ◇KQ. So finessing a diamond would be a dumb move. East would win and clear hearts.

At trick two, Ukarde played a confident ♠K. When West ducked, Ukarde placed a low spade on the table, neatly severing the defenders' communications. The diamond merchant's look of surprise as he won the cheap trick changed to one of high anxiety as the implications dawned on him. Correctly suspecting that, if he cashed his ♠A, declarer would have nine cold tricks, he fired his best shot, the ♡K. The super-safe Ukarde ducked smoothly, won the third round of the suit on the table, and called for the ◇10. This was covered by East for the defence's third trick.

With only minor suits left, the palooka exited with a club. Ukarde won in hand, and smartly led his remaining diamond to the knave. East had nowhere to hide. He won the trick, but now dummy's ♣Q provided an entry to the long diamonds. Ukarde had made a spade, two hearts, two clubs and four diamonds.

The quality of the dummy play was lost on East, who glared resentfully at his partner.

"It should never make against best defence," he complained.

"Please forgive me for contradicting you, sir," Ukarde murmured deferentially, "but I believe I did receive the best defence."

"My partner could have switched to a club."

"He could," agreed Ukarde. "But then the ace of hearts would have provided my entry to the table."

"Well, if you know so much, how come you never made your ace-king of clubs?"

"You are quite right, sir." Ukarde gave his forehead a rueful slap. "It was very careless of me."

Ukarde's partner decided to join in. Bugatti was a vast, genial, dangerous man. He owned half the rackets in Morocco, for which he had mortgaged half of his soul to the Devil. It was no secret that he would have given the other half to own Brick's American Bar.

"Perhaps we should ask our distinguished host to adjudicate," Bugatti chuckled. "Mr Lane never plays bridge, but he talks the best game I have ever heard. Maestro, how should our friends have defended?"

"It was so long ago, I can't remember," said Brick, who found post-mortems as unproductive as funerals.

"But, Brick," the loser in the East seat was a serial masochist. "At least tell them that I made no mistake."

"Not until you opened your mouth," Brick conceded. "It turned the suspicion that you were a palooka into a sure bet."

Everybody laughed. Brick's insults were part of the floor show. And they always came back for more.

Bugatti was laughing loudest. "Brick, you have just confirmed what I have always suspected. The secret of your establishment's success is your irresistible New World charm."

"But the establishment's still not for sale, Bugatti," Brick told him. "And you can't have Slam either. He's my indentured bond-servant."

The next deal was as dull as a widow's axe, and Brick walked over to his private table, where Carl, the head waiter, had laid out the day's bridge problem. Brick liked problems. They helped you whittle away a slice of your life, without having to put up with people you didn't respect, which in Brick's case was nearly everyone. He spotted Carl and showed him three fingers. Carl moseyed off and returned, bearing a large bourbon, and clucking like a mother hen over her favourite chick.

"Monsieur Brick," he remonstrated, "you are getting to be your best customer. Wouldn't you prefer a black coffee?"

"If I'd wanted coffee, I'd have said so. Three fingers mean a bourbon. Coffee is seven toes and a left buttock." Brick took a Homeric swallow. "And don't wet nurse me, you cuddly Dutchman. This is only my second drink of the evening."

"I know. But your first drink was a quart of bourbon." Carl gave his head a censorious shake, sending his plump cheeks and two of his chins into a protracted wobble.

Brick held up three defiant fingers. "Hit me again, Carl. I can never solve bridge problems while I'm sober. And I can still lie on the floor without holding on."

Carl wagged his head again, but not critically; he was just returning his face to its original shape. He was halfway through the process when Ukarde arrived.

"Hello, Brick," he smiled meekly. "May I join you?" He sat down, beating Brick's no by a split second. "It was amazing the way you stood up to the Deutsche Bank just now."

"It was amazing he could stand up at all," said Carl, and waddled off with the air of a man who knew an exit line when he said one.

♠ J1072
♡ 10652
◇ Q6542
♣ -

♠ AQ
♡ AKJ
◇ AK87
♣ AKJ10

Ukarde lit a cigarette as he took in the two hands. "Six no trumps?" he enquired politely.

"So I'm told."

"And may I ask what was led?"

"The diamond knave. But I don't need any helpful hints for greenhorns."

"Of course not, Brick. There is a rumour that in the bridge salons of Paris you had quite a reputation."

"There's a rumour that Hitler dines nightly at Rosenblum's Delicatessen, but I wouldn't bet the farm on it."

"That reminds me. Wasn't it a shame about those two German agents? The poor devils."

"They got lucky, Ukarde. Yesterday they were a couple of no-account spies. Today they're enjoying a ride with the Valkyries."

"I hope so." Ukarde nodded compassionately. "Have you noticed that unless the opposing diamonds are divided two-two, the suit is blocked?"

"Ukarde, one more crack like that and you'll join the Deutsche Bank in the john."

"I'm sorry, Brick. I never know when to keep my mouth shut. I'm afraid I am my own worst enemy."

"Don't be too sure, Ukarde. You've got a lot of competition."

Ukarde gave him a sharp look. "You despise me, don't you?" he asked.

"If I thought about you I probably would."

For a few moments Ukarde looked as sad as a homeless tapeworm. Then he recovered, and scanned the room for eavesdroppers. There were only six, which in Casablanca was an acute shortage.

"Perhaps because you despise you are the only one I can trust," he said. "Have you heard about the new German Meistersystem with its eighty-one conventions?"

"Who hasn't? In the villages of Morocco they talk of little else. But I thought the number was seventy-nine."

"That was this morning. Brick, the Austrians won the World Championship using the system of Paul Stern, a Jew. Imagine what an embarrassment that was to the Master Race. So what do you think they did?"

"Made Stern an honorary gentile?"

"Even better. From nowhere they produced a miracle the all-singing, all-dancing von Erheim system, in a book back-dated to prove that Stern snatched his ideas."

"Ukarde," Brick sighed, "I hope that a punch line is lurking somewhere in the middle distance."

Ukarde produced a fat wad of papers. "These prove beyond doubt that Stern conceived his system before von Erheim had even heard of bridge. Letters from publishers and bridge experts all over the world, and all originals. They pre-date even the Gestapo's pre-dating."

Brick flicked through the papers. "Well, Ukarde," he said, "I'm beginning to despise you a little less. I heard those two dead agents were looking for a mysterious dossier."

"I heard that rumour too. Brick, I can sell these for a king's ransom. But I need you to hide them for me."

"For how long?"

"Just tonight. And my customer will call for me this evening. Will you tell him he can find me in the bridge room?"

"What's his name? Or is that a military secret?"

"It's no secret. His name is Victor Hilo."

The habitually bored expression vanished from Brick's face. "Victor Hilo?" he asked.

"Brick, you almost sound impressed. Have you heard of him?"

"Everyone in bridge has heard of him. He's one of the great players. They've even named a defensive signal after him."

Ukarde's brow furrowed as he tried to recall all the defensive signals. "Of course," he said. "The Victor Echo. Did you know he is the leader of the resistance movement?"

"Against the Nazis?"

"Against the von Erheim system. Brick, I cannot thank you enough. In return, I have some valuable information for you." He leaned forward conspiratorially. "Play the spade queen at trick two." He grinned, and was off as quick as a bride's nightgown.

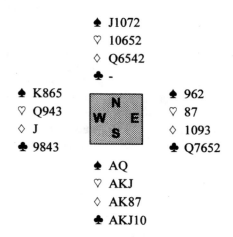

Brick exposed the East-West hands. The little man was right. Running the ♠Q was the key play. Whichever defender took the trick, declarer could win any return, cash the ♠A, and play two more rounds of clubs, finishing on the table. Now he could unblock the diamond suit by parking his nine on dummy's ♠J, and claim.

Then Carl returned, with another drink and some unwanted advice. "Have you decided what to do if the defenders refuse to take their king of spades?" he asked.

"Yes," Brick told him, through gritted teeth.

"Good," Carl nodded. He placed Brick's empty glass on his tray, and flicked some imaginary crumbs from the table. "Of course a master like you would immediately play his knave of hearts."

"In sleep," Brick yawned.

"I knew it!" Carl clucked with pleasure. "Then, if they ducked, you would have five major suit tricks in the bag. And you would only need three clubs and four diamonds for your contract."

"Yes, Carl, I can count up to twelve without your help."

"And if they didn't duck, you would "

"I'd win the return, cash my top hearts, play two rounds of clubs, and dump my diamond nine on one of dummy's heart winners. Then I'd grab the Dutch lame-brain who fixed this deal, and tell him to stop giving me baby problems and watered-down drinks."

Carl wandered off, beaming like a man who knew he was loved and appreciated. Brick finished his drink, stuffed the Stern papers into his tuxedo, and went down to the saloon. He eased casually towards Slam's piano, and furtively slipped them under the lid.

"Hi, Boss," Slam greeted him. "That Ukarde man's been lookin' for you."

"I know, Slam. He found me."

Slam's face began to crease with irritation, as he ran his fingers over the top octaves. "Boss," he said, "would you mind movin' Ukarde's papers further down the piano. They're givin' a tinny sound to the upper registers."

Brick swore under his breath. "Slam," he groaned wearily, "you'll just have to play in a lower key. It'll be a good chance to do your Satchmo impression."

Suddenly, the door of the card room flew open, and a desperate Ukarde emerged, firing pistol shots at a posse of pursuing gendarmes.

"Brick, help me!" he cried.

"Don't be a fool, Ukarde. You can't get away."

"Brick, you've got to hide me!"

"Give yourself up, Ukarde. Your only hope is to plead insanity. I'll be your expert witness."

Ukarde was dragged off, struggling like a madman. Brick shrugged his shoulders and was on his way to the bar, when Louis Delage intercepted him.

"Thank you for not interfering," he said. "I should have hated to arrest my best friend."

"I know, Louis. And the sight of your tears of sorrow would have broken my heart."

Louis turned triumphantly to Strafe, who was sitting at his table. "You see, Major? You have no need to worry about Brick; he is completely neutral. Brick, let me introduce you to Major Heinrich Strafe."

Strafe rose imperiously. "Please join us, Mr Lane"

Brick eyed the major with his well-rehearsed neutral expression. "Thank you," he said neutrally.

"I have heard a great deal about you," said Strafe. "Do you mind if I ask you a few questions?"

"Why not? I might even answer them."

"What is your nationality?"

"I'm a drunkard."

"When I first heard of you I assumed you were English. Our agents in England tell me that Brick Lane is a seedy little street in London's East End."

"It is. I understand that it was named after me. But I was born in New York."

"Are you by any chance Jewish?"

"I wasn't the last time I looked."

Strafe made a note. "I know that you came here from Paris," he said.

Brick nodded. "I left when the German army arrived. The town wasn't big enough for the both of us."

"That was wise of you. We have a complete dossier about you from Military Intelligence."

"Military Intelligence?" Brick looked puzzled. "Isn't that a contradiction in terms?"

Louis laughed. Strafe did not.

"An enemy of the Reich has come to Casablanca," he said. "Your past record suggests you might be disposed to help him."

"Brick has changed since then," Louis interceded. "I like to think I have had a good influence on him, and I'm sure his misguided idealism has withered in the desert air. Nowadays he sticks his neck out for nobody."

"Not even for Victor Hilo?" Strafe was sceptical. "He is reputed to be a fine card player and, according to our agents in Paris, Mr Lane is another."

"But his bidding is a trifle wild for your taste, Major," said Louis.

"So I am told." Strafe consulted his notebook. "In Paris, Mr Lane, you were heard to say artificial conventions were the last refuge of the bridge idiot."

"I'm sorry. I should have said dummkopf."

"Have you read von Erheim's *Design for Bidding*?"

"If I wanted to read a bridge book, Major, I would write one."

"But you were referring to the von Erheim system?"

"Not especially; it isn't all bad. It whiles away the time. I'm told it takes nine rounds of bidding to reach a partscore."

"So Hilo's lies have reached Casablanca. Three times he has slipped through our fingers. Before his last escape, we persuaded him to take part in a match against a top German team." He took a sheet of paper from his pocket. "Observe the superb precision of the von Erheim auction."

Game All. Dealer East.

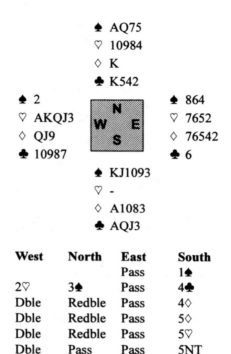

```
                    ♠ AQ75
                    ♡ 10984
                    ◇ K
                    ♣ K542
  ♠ 2                              ♠ 864
  ♡ AKQJ3                          ♡ 7652
  ◇ QJ9                            ◇ 76542
  ♣ 10987                          ♣ 6
                    ♠ KJ1093
                    ♡ -
                    ◇ A1083
                    ♣ AQJ3
```

West	North	East	South
		Pass	1♠
2♡	3♣	Pass	4♣
Dble	Redble	Pass	4◇
Dble	Redble	Pass	5◇
Dble	Redble	Pass	5♡
Dble	Pass	Pass	5NT
Dble	7♠	Pass	Pass
Dble	Pass	Pass	Redble
All Pass			

Brick stared at the tortuous auction with an expression of unsuspended disbelief.

"All South's bids after his initial opening were asking bids," Strafe explained. "You appear to be ignorant of the device."

"Blissfully. But why did West double everything in sight?"

"Apparently doubling was an emotional outlet. He did not like Germans."

"There's no accounting for taste," Brick sympathised.

"Quite," said Strafe. "And his aggression did him no good whatsoever. It enabled North to demonstrate the renowned von Erheim redouble. His first two showed second round control. His third showed third round control."

"You don't say," Brick drawled. "Now correct me if I'm wrong, Major, but I guess all South now needed to know was the quality of his partner's spade holding."

"True," Strafe agreed.

"Then why the pointless five heart bid?"

"A good question. He was convinced that West would double again, as indeed he did. Now North was able to execute a von Erheim pass, showing no heart control."

"But South was void in the suit," Brick persisted. "He didn't need to be told his partner had a few small hearts."

"Of course not," Strafe said. "He was toying with his opponents, to prove that we Germans have a sense of humour." He gave a hollow laugh, to reinforce his claim. "His five no trump bid was a return to reality, a grand slam force. Holding two of the top spade honours, North bid seven with complete confidence."

"Then why didn't he find a confident redouble?" Brick asked.

"Protocol," explained Strafe. "As the junior partner, he correctly left that honour to South."

There was a profound silence. It was broken by Louis, as soon as he could trust himself to speak. "Major, I must congratulate you. The auction demonstrates all the great Nazi virtues; precision, courage, flair, flexibility..."

"And chutzpah," Brick added.

"I do not understand," said Strafe. "What is chutzpah?"

"It is an old Bavarian word, Major," Louis lied smoothly. "Roughly translated, it means 'audacity'."

"For the record, how did the auction go in the other room?" asked Brick.

"It was a travesty," Strafe snarled. "Hilo was North. He and his partner ignored West's overcall. They bid one spade, four spades, six spades, seven spades."

"Barbaric!" said Louis.

"And when our West doubled on principle, they had the chutzpah to redouble." Strafe pronounced the Yiddish word with linguistic pride. He could not wait to use it at the next Gestapo clam-bake.

"So it was a flat board?" said Brick flatly.

"But a moral victory for our side," said Strafe.

"In a pig's ear," said Brick.

"What do you mean?" Strafe demanded.

"Another Bavarian expression," said Louis hastily.

"After that sequence, seven spades was a standout," Brick stated. "When a pair needs six rounds of mumbo jumbo to reach an easy grand like that, it's a marvel one of them doesn't drop dead from exhaustion."

"So!" Strafe was not pleased. "You are just another blundering American, and a back number, like your soul-mate, Hilo. He has a prominent place on our black list. Do not be surprised if one day your name is next to his."

"Thanks for the compliment." Brick stood up with what he hoped was massive dignity. "I used to have a capacity for being surprised. But I left it behind in Paris. And now, if you'll excuse me, Major, I have a saloon to run."

Chapter Three

A few minutes after Brick left Major Strafe, every eye in the saloon turned to marvel at the woman who had just entered. You could have put a Gershwin tune to a Shakespeare sonnet and it still would not have done her justice. She was Lisa, the toast of all the bridge joints in all the towns in all the world. And now she had to walk into Brick's.

At her side was a tall man in a gleaming white suit. White looked well on Victor Hilo. He was an idealist, a hero, a messiah, and he believed in dressing for the part.

There was a tense moment as they passed Slam the pianist. Lisa turned as white as Victor's suit, and Slam played a string of wrong notes, which the audience took to be modern jazz, and applauded knowingly.

Victor noticed nothing. They sat down. He ordered two Cointreaus. Later he would drink champagne, champagne cocktails and brandy. To a resistance leader, mixing booze was a very minor hazard.

"Victor, I'm worried," said Lisa. "Everyone is staring in our direction."

"I know." Victor's eyes twinkled. "It always happens when I wear this suit."

"But the place is full of Germans."

"So, I believe was Berlin. Yet I escaped. I've been in difficult spots before."

"Like the time you bid that no trump slam with two aces missing?"

"And made an overtrick, darling. Never forget that."

A mysterious stranger appeared at their table. He glanced around furtively, and sat down.

"Excuse me," he whispered. "But I am forced to sell this ring. I wondered..."

"Thank you, " Victor was courteous, but firm. "But I am not in the jewellery business."

"It is not an ordinary ring, Monsieur. Let me show you." The stranger pressed a secret catch. The top of the ring flew open, to reveal a miniature playing card. The card was the queen of hearts; the face of the queen was Lisa's. It was the sign of the resistance movement.

"Yes, I am very interested," said Victor. "Where can we meet?"

"In five minutes time, at the bar." He lowered his voice. "I am glad you are alive, Monsieur. I heard three separate rumours that you had been killed."

"I heard them too. They were so convincing I almost believed them. By the way, I am supposed to meet a man called Ukarde. Do you know where I can find him?"

"Probably in a prison cell. He was arrested a few minutes ago."

The stranger vanished, and was immediately replaced by Louis. Things moved fast at Brick's.

"Monsieur Hilo, is it not?" Louis was the soul of affability.

"I do not deny it."

"I am Captain Louis Delage. As Prefect of Police, may I welcome you to Casablanca?"

"You are most gracious."

"Not at all." Louis gazed with frank admiration at Lisa. "I heard a rumour – perhaps one should call it an understatement – of your remarkable elegance."

"You are very kind," Victor thawed appreciably. "But without the suit I am really quite ordinary."

"Captain," said Lisa. "The man who owns this bar, Brick. I think I know him. What is he like?"

"Brick? He is the kind of man who wins the fight, the girl and the glory. If I were a woman, and I were not around, Brick is the kind of man I should fall in love with. Does that sound strange to you?"

"Not at all," Lisa reassured him. "We have a lot of friends who are that way inclined."

The next to arrive was Strafe, who towered over them with a menacing air

"Good evening," he bowed ironically. "This is an honour I have long looked forward to."

"I have no idea who you are." Victor was supremely calm. "But it is an honour I would prefer to avoid." He stood up to look his adversary in the face. Each strove to look taller than the other – it was a dead heat.

Louis coughed discreetly. "I should explain that Major Strafe is one of the Gestapo's rising stars. "A few years ago he was unknown in Germany. And now…"

"And now he is unknown throughout the world," said Victor.

"You are very sharp, Herr Hilo. I will be blunt." Strafe's stare could have opened a can of sauerkraut at twelve paces. "Three times you have eluded us. Now you have come to Casablanca. It is my intention to see that you stay in Casablanca."

"Good intentions are all very well, Major. But remember that the road to Hell is paved with them."

"Now I understand your reputation for eloquence," said Strafe. "You have a cliché for every occasion."

"The Major is quite right," said Louis. "To impress an expert such as he, you will need some new clichés. I shall let you have a list."

"Thank you, but I have already read *Mein Kampf*. And I would prefer a pair of exit visas."

"I would like to help you," Louis sighed. "But in our harmonious partnership with the Third Reich, I am afraid the Vichy government is…"

"Is a minority shareholder; I am well aware of it," said Victor. He sat down, and Strafe, taking this as an admission of defeat, followed his example. "Of course," he said, "under certain circumstances we might arrange for you and your charming companion to spend the rest of the war in America. You are the leader of the resistance. All you would have to do is give us the names of all its members."

"I can do better than that, Major. I can tell you an infallible way to identify them. Your supporters bid like puppets on a string pulled from Berlin. And every time they make an artificial bid their noses grow longer. My people bid like bridge players."

"I see." Strafe could barely control his fury. "Then you may remain in

Casablanca for the rest of your life. And I suspect it will not be a long one." He marched off, with Louis in his wake.

Victor placed his hand on Lisa's. "In a revolution, one wins or dies," he smiled. "If so, let me be buried with a gun in my hand, standing upright, and facing Germany."

"Of course, Victor. And in your white suit. I will see to it."

"Thank you." He glanced at his watch. "After Ukarde's arrest there is nothing to keep us here. I have an appointment at the bar. The mysterious stranger may know a way to get exit visas. And I am beginning to feel crowded at this table. It is like the Gare du Nord on a Friday afternoon."

"Be careful, Victor." Her voice was full of concern. "And on your way would you ask the pianist to come here?"

Victor walked towards the bar, mildly perplexed that this time nobody gave him a second glance. Lisa was left alone; but not for long. An upright piano appeared, pushed by a perspiring Slam.

"It has been a long time, Slam," she said.

"I'm sorry, Miss Lisa, but this piano ain't easy to push."

"I meant since Paris."

"Yes, ma'am. A lot of water under the bridge."

"Yes. I shall never forget the Seine. Play some of the old songs, Slam."

Slam began to improvise, carefully avoiding the top register, and any tune that remotely resembled the forbidden *As Time Goes By*.

"Where is Brick?" she asked shyly.

"Leave him alone, Miss Lisa. You're bad luck to him."

"Play it, Slam," she said. "For old time's sake."

"I don't know what you mean, Miss Lisa."

"Play *As Time Goes By*."

Slam knew it was no use arguing. All men were putty in Lisa's hands. He began to play and sing:

> *You must remember this:*
> *A kiss is still a kiss*
> *A sigh is just a sigh...*

"Not those words, Slam. The special ones you wrote for me after Brick and I won the Versailles Mixed Pairs."

"I don't remember that version, Miss Lisa."

"It doesn't matter; I have it here. With a copy of that final hand, the hand I'll never forget."

She took two tattered pages from her purse, and gave one to Slam. A tear fell onto the other as she gazed at it. It was the record of her greatest triumph, the magic moment when she won the right to call herself a bridge player. They were playing the reigning champions, Monsieur and Madame Dupont.

Love All. Dealer South.

Mme Dupont
♠ 94
♡ KJ9
◇ Q1095
♣ QJ93

Brick
♠ Q10752
♡ 87
◇ 843
♣ 875

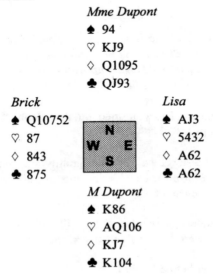

Lisa
♠ AJ3
♡ 5432
◇ A62
♣ A62

M Dupont
♠ K86
♡ AQ106
◇ KJ7
♣ K104

West	North	East	South
			1NT
Pass	2NT	Pass	3NT
All Pass			

Lead: ♣2

Slam's throaty voice rang out with the immortal words which had recorded her defence for posterity:

> *Your partner led the two.*
> *You wondered what to do,*
> *And sighed a little sigh.*
> *The good old rule of third hand high*
> *Might not apply.*

> *And when you chose the knave*
> *Declarer's face turned grave*
> *He had no safe reply.*
> *And as he played the king, his chance*
> *Passed sadly by.*

Her tears were flowing freely as Slam reached the highly-charged middle section:

> *Your clever knave had sealed poor Dupont's fate.*
> *He should have ducked, but now it was too late.*
> *Needing nine tricks, he ended up with eight.*
> *The score sheet doesn't lie...*

At that climactic moment, Brick stormed into the saloon. "Slam," he snarled. "I told you never to play that..."

His voice faded as he saw Lisa. As Slam guiltily shunted his piano away, Brick's face contorted with a bewildering mixture of emotions – passion, jealousy, and perhaps even a touch of hate.

He was dragged rudely to earth by the silky voice of Louis Delage. "Mademoiselle, you were asking about Brick, and here he is. May I..."

"Brick and I have met before," said Lisa.

"Have you indeed? Then let me to introduce him to Monsieur Victor Hilo."

Brick nodded. For him that was a sign of deep respect. "Congratulations," he said.

"Thank you," said Victor. "But what for?"

"Your dummy play, your flawless defence, the superb simplicity of your bidding."

Victor bowed in acknowledgement. "I congratulate you in return. Your tribute had the two essential qualities of a Hilo auction: economy and accuracy. Will you join us?"

"Of course."

"A precedent!" Louis exclaimed. "Brick never drinks with his customers."

"Then we are privileged," said Victor. "Are you a keen player, Monsieur Lane?"

"I used to fool around at the game."

"Brick is being modest," Lisa broke in. "He and I won the Versailles Mixed Pairs."

"Really?" Victor was clearly surprised. He turned towards Brick. "Were the Duponts playing?"

"They were. I remember every detail. The Duponts wore grey; Lisa wore blue."

"Yes," she smiled serenely, hoping that nobody could hear the way her heart was beating. "I have put that dress away. I may wear it again when Victor lets me partner him in a tournament."

"Lisa, there will be time enough for that when our struggle is victorious." She tried to interrupt, but nothing short of an earthquake could stop Victor in full flow. "All over Europe, freedom-loving bridge players meet in underground cellars to share the joys of natural bidding. Soon they will rise from those cellars to play in small back rooms. Then, as our numbers grow, every town and village will ring with our battle cry – *One spade, Four spades, Six spades, Pass!* And as each group is brutally gunned down, two more will take its place. Even Nazis can't kill that fast."

The silence was awesome. Victor's recruiting speech may have been short on sales appeal, but nobody could find words to express the emotions it had aroused.

Except Lisa. "Victor," she cried. "You always make that speech when I want you to play in a tournament with me. If you had seen the hand I defended against the Duponts... Wait, I have it here!" She proudly displayed the much-thumbed page. "I have never dared to show it to you before. I was afraid you wouldn't believe me."

"Lisa," Brick warned her, "I don't think this is the time..."

It was too late. Victor had analysed the deal with bewildering speed. "I see the two of spades was led," he observed. "Lisa, you contributed your knave of course?"

"Yes." She tried desperately to conceal her anguish as he casually designated her master-stroke as commonplace.

"And naturally Dupont won the trick?" Victor looked at Lisa, who nodded eagerly. "One down," he said, smiling his approval.

"Yes," she replied hopefully. "It won us the championship."

"Congratulations, Monsieur Lane. Your deuce was an inspired lead. Having no re-entry outside the spade suit, it was your only hope. Poor Dupont. Believing the spades to be equally divided, he saw no point in ducking."

"But, Victor..." Lisa began.

"You too, Lisa." He gave her head a paternal pat. "You play was...correct. It reminds me of a similar situation, but a far more difficult one."

He began to scribble on the back of Lisa's precious sheet of paper, blissfully unaware that, to her, this was an act of desecration, like drawing a moustache on the *Mona Lisa*.

"I sat East," he said. "My partner was a fine defender. Our opponents were scientific bidders, though not quite in the von Erheim mould."

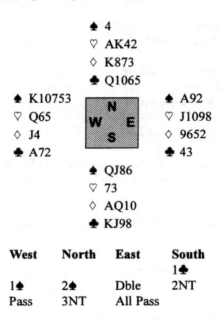

```
                    ♠ 4
                    ♡ AK42
                    ◇ K873
                    ♣ Q1065
   ♠ K10753                        ♠ A92
   ♡ Q65          N                ♡ J1098
   ◇ J4        W     E             ◇ 9652
   ♣ A72          S                ♣ 43
                    ♠ QJ86
                    ♡ 73
                    ◇ AQ10
                    ♣ KJ98
```

West	North	East	South
			1♣
1♠	2♠	Dble	2NT
Pass	3NT	All Pass	

"North's two spade bid was a game force," Victor told them. "It said nothing about his spade holding. West led the five of spades." He paused didactically. "What card should I play?"

Louis was the first to speak. "The nine," he said confidently.

"But why?"

"Because, Professor, it is the only card to beat the contract."

"As the cards lie," Victor agreed. "But suppose West had led from…"

♠ QJ853

Lisa moaned as he compounded his vandalism by penning the alternative holding on her tear-stained treasure. It was as if he had added a beard to the moustache:

Louis was unabashed. "In that case I should naturally play my ace and return the nine to clear the suit." he announced shamelessly.

"Captain Delage, your bridge is like your politics. You blow with the wind. Perhaps Monsieur Lane is less inclined to sit on the fence."

"Perhaps," said Brick. "You said West was a fine player. With that holding a lot of experts, knowing that declarer had a spade stopper, would lead the queen. That's why East should play the nine."

"It is a matter of opinion," said Louis.

"Most things in bridge are a matter of opinion," said Victor, "but I agree with Monsieur Lane." He glanced at his watch. "Lisa, I hate to be the one to say it, but it is getting late."

"You're right," said Louis. "We must observe the curfew. I will get you a taxi."

"Goodnight, Monsieur Lane." Victor rose. "We must play together some time."

"But Brick never plays ... " began Louis.

"Thanks," Brick interrupted him. "Maybe we'll do that."

"Another precedent," Louis remarked thoughtfully, and left to summon the cab.

"Give my regards to Slam," said Lisa. "Tell him nobody plays *As Time Goes By* like he does. But I will never ask him to sing that lyric again. The words have lost their meaning."

When everyone had gone, Brick stood for a moment, gazing after them with his basset-hound eyes. Then he slowly mounted the stairs to his room above the saloon.

He needed a drink.

Chapter Four

It was three o'clock in the morning, and Brick had the saloon to himself. He slumped moodily over a table, with a bottle in one hand and a glass in the other. He gripped them like a dying man clutching at his life support system, until Slam emerged from the dark shadows and stood beside the piano, watching him sadly.

"Boss," he said. "Are you going to bed?"

"No."

"Ain't you ever going to bed?"

"I'm waiting for a woman. I don't care how long it takes. I know she'll come."

Slam opened the piano lid, took out Ukarde's papers and put them on Brick's table. Then he sat down and began to play.

"Boss," he said. "Let's get away from here. We can go fishin'."

"That's a good offer, Slam. Do you mind if I drink it over?"

"You oughta lay off the bottle, Mr Brick. You're lookin' terrible. Your voice is slurred, your eyes are bloodshot…"

"If you think they're bloodshot you should see 'em from this side." Brick topped up his glass defiantly. "Play it, Slam. You played it for her; you can play it for me. But don't sing those goddam words."

Sam gave his famous rendition of *As Time Goes By*, while Brick tormented himself with memories of Paris…Lisa's lovely face. Her sweet voice when she first told him, "*Je t'aime*." The way his heart leaped when he thumbed through his French dictionary and discovered what it meant. The way the earth moved when they made love, as if the Eiffel Tower had finally met the Arc de Triomphe

He pictured their first game of bridge together, at the *Belle Aurore*. Their French opponents were anonymous, and deserve to remain so.

Love All. Dealer South.

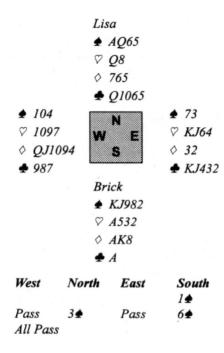

Lisa
♠ AQ65
♡ Q8
◊ 765
♣ Q1065

♠ 104   ♠ 73
♡ 1097   ♡ KJ64
◊ QJ1094   ◊ 32
♣ 987   ♣ KJ432

Brick
♠ KJ982
♡ A532
◊ AK8
♣ A

West	North	East	South
			1♠
Pass	3♠	Pass	6♠
All Pass			

After winning the lead of the ◊Q in hand, Brick could see that if the ♡K was onside, the slam was a virtual milk run. But he wanted to look good in front of Lisa. He lit a cigarette while he tried to figure an extra edge. Maybe the club king would fall in three rounds. Or East might hold both outstanding honours and decide to split them. A club had to be led from dummy, but which one? The queen would be a spectacular choice, but the bridge columns were full of plays like that, and Lisa looked like a girl who devoured bridge columns for breakfast.

He took a deep breath of therapeutic smoke, played his ♠8 to dummy's ♠A, and called for the ♣10. Like a true gentleman, East covered with the knave. Brick crossed to the ♠Q and continued with a low club from the table. When East produced the king, Brick wanted to give him a medal. Instead, managing to look bored, he ruffed, drew trumps and claimed.

"How could I guess your ace was singleton?" asked his bemused opponent. "Naturally I assumed you had the nine and were trying to sneak a trick."

"It was a logical assumption," said Brick. It wasn't, of course, but Brick was in a grateful mood. His barnstorming play would never have succeeded against good defence: even a half-awake West would have given count. Against good defenders, the only chance was to lead a low club from dummy on the first round. It would then be reasonable for East to split, on the basis that declarer's holding might be:

♠ *KJ982*
♡ *A*
◊ *AK984*
♣ *A9*

But he could see that Lisa was impressed. Her eyes shone with admiration as he lifted his champagne glass in a victory salute.

"Here's looking at you, kid," he said...

◊ ◊ ◊ ◊ ◊

As he remembered the warmth of her smile, Brick's eyes grew moist – it must have been the smoke from his cigarette. Now he recalled the spine-tingling moment when she agreed to come with him to Marseilles, and the agony of waiting on the station platform with a comical look on his face, and his insides kicked to pieces, when he realised he'd been dumped.

He banged his glass on the table, but his luck was out – it refused to break. Badly needing a distraction, he idly browsed through Ukarde's papers.

"Why didn't she show up at the station, Slam?" he asked.

"Don't ask me, Boss."

"And stop calling me Boss."

"Yes, Boss."

"Can you figure women out, Slam?"

"No, Boss. It's like trying to figure out a trump squeeze. I gave up years ago."

"You never said a truer word, Slam. Trying to figure out a woman is like doing a jigsaw puzzle without the picture."

"I don't know why you bother, Mr Brick."

"I can't resist the curvy bits, Slam."

"I know the feeling, Boss."

"Do you want a drink?"

"No thanks. You're doin' enough drinkin' for both of us."

"Know something, Slam? Lisa and Victor and me – we're stuck in Casablanca till the end of time. We're all on the black list."

"Welcome to the club, Boss."

Suddenly Brick froze. He'd seen something in Ukarde's papers which swept like a cleansing wind through the drunken haze. Then Slam stopped playing, as he stared towards the doorway. Painfully, Brick swivelled his own eyes in the same direction. And slowly, they focused on Lisa.

"Brick," she whispered. "I couldn't help myself. I had to come."

"Why?" he asked, hoarsely.

"To tell you that when we walked into your saloon I had no idea you were the owner."

"I guess the sign *Brick's American Bar* was a pretty obscure clue," he said. "Slam, would you mind leaving us?"

"Slam has already gone, my darling," said Lisa, in a voice you could have poured on a waffle.

"I didn't hear him," said Brick, in a voice that could have grated a nutmeg.

"He left his piano behind," she explained.

Brick ground out his cigarette so furiously that he missed the ashtray by a good foot. "Why weren't you at the station, Lisa?" he growled.

"When I fell in love with you in Paris, I believed my husband was dead. Only that morning I learned he was still alive."

"You should have told me, Lisa."

"I couldn't. We had to keep our marriage a secret. You see, my husband is Victor Hilo."

Brick's face was a study of passion, hate, and maybe a touch of jealousy. "Victor Hilo!" he echoed.

"Yes. If the Gestapo knew I was his wife, they would have him in their power. To save me from torture, death, or a fate nearly as bad…"

"I get the picture," Brick snapped. "Are you in love with him?"

"In a way. He is like a father to me. I look up to him."

"He's very tall."

"I know. And sometimes he makes me feel very small. You saw him earlier, showing his silly little girl that it was not she who defeated the Duponts, but you, Brick, with your 'inspired' deuce of spades, convincing them that the spades were four-four …"

"Now don't sell yourself short, Lisa. Your knave helped."

"But I hadn't even noticed that you'd led fifth highest." She moved closer to him. "And you, Brick, you let me cherish my illusions. You even told Sam to write my song. If I didn't have a million other reasons for loving you, I would love you for that alone."

Brick took her in his arms. He'd made himself a promise that he wouldn't, but there were a million reasons for breaking it. A minute passed, or it may have been a week.

"It's a great story, Lisa," he said. "But it doesn't have a finish."

Their lips met. They had met before, in Paris, but not like this.

A lifetime later, Lisa spoke. Her voice was like old Madeira, made audible. "You must write that finish. Do the thinking for both of us. My heart tells me I must leave Victor, but then I remember how much he needs me, how much I owe to him. I remember those wonderful, endless nights, when he lay beside me and told me about all his famous hands. I remember…"

"You've made the point, Lisa – you've got a hell of a memory." Brick walked to the table. "Here are the papers Ukarde meant for Victor. And there's a bonus, two letters of transit, signed by General de Gaulle. Two passports to freedom, which cannot be rescinded, or even questioned."

"Brick!" she gasped. "I can't believe it."

"There's a snag, Lisa." He poured another drink. "A problem in higher mathematics."

"What is it, Brick?"

He held up the letters. "Three into two won't go," he said. He raised his glass.

"Here's looking at you, kid."

Chapter Five

Next morning, Louis received a visit from Strafe. The major was on the warpath, and the Frenchman was his prime target.

"Captain, you have blundered." He looked down at Louis as though he was an unpleasant stain on the carpet. "Ukarde's death was a severe setback to my plans."

"I imagine it was rather a setback to Ukarde's."

"You say he was shot while trying to escape?"

"Or committed suicide. I haven't decided which."

"A pity. I had planned a more protracted end for him, preceded by a revealing conversation on the whereabouts of the Stern papers."

"I don't doubt it," Louis grimaced.

"You are playing a dangerous game, Captain. I sometimes wonder which side you are on."

"I blow with the wind, Major. And the prevailing wind blows from Berlin, via Vichy."

"Never forget that." Strafe relaxed, but only a trifle. "I am convinced Ukarde gave the papers to Herr Lane. You searched his place thoroughly?"

"With a fine toothcomb."

"Perhaps an axe would have been more effective. By now those documents could be anywhere. Do you think he would part with them – at a price?"

"I doubt it. I hate to speak ill of a friend, Major, but, underneath that cynical veneer, Brick is a romantic."

"I see. Is he a gambler?"

"On occasion."

"Very interesting. Perhaps I should get to know him better. Field Marshal Rommel says that time spent in reconnaissance is seldom wasted. Do you think he might be tempted by an intriguing contest of rubber bridge?"

"I think you'll find that he's too busy with the Africa Corps." Louis remarked, and relished the scowl on Strafe's face. "Oh, you mean Brick," he added innocently. "Yes, he might." He exhaled a reflective cloud of cigarette smoke. "I suspect he would give his eye teeth to partner a great player – like Victor Hilo."

"You pronounce his name as though you greatly admire him."

"I suppose I do, Major. Despite the fact that he has no redeeming defect, one cannot help worshipping the quicksand he walks on."

"I admit he has courage. And he would not be able to resist such a challenge. We bested him before, but I will concede that the team-mates we provided for him were..."

"Carefully vetted?"

"Exactly."

"For their politics rather than their bridge?"

"Of course. It was not playing the game, but I have observed that people who play the game will usually lose it. However, this time we will provide a level playing field. I will have a top German star flown in, and with our Meistersystem we will be invincible."

"Unstoppable."

"Thank you, Captain." Strafe stood up. Louis sensed there was a speech coming, but he could think of no way to prevent it. "Can you imagine our triumph when we destroy that demigod in front of his disciples? Those refugees will be utterly demoralised. They will crawl back to occupied Europe, with their spirits broken, their heads bowed, and their tails between their legs."

"You think they'll be a trifle upset?"

"I do. And during their journey home they will master the von Erheim system, or we will hear the reason why."

"It might have something to do with its complexity, Major. But now you must excuse me. I have a bridge game to arrange."

◇ ◇ ◇ ◇ ◇

"Shall we play a weak no trump?" asked Victor.

"Why not?" Brick agreed, as he poured two antique cognacs.

"And weak jump overcalls?"

"The weaker the better."

"Agreed. Anything to deprive them of bidding space."

"Yes, Victor," said Brick evenly. "The penny had actually dropped."

"I'm sorry. I'm afraid I often preach to the converted. It is a bad habit."

"Have another brandy. It will help you kick it."

They were in Brick's private office, making a hole in his private stock. Victor took a sheet of paper from the desk, and wrote out the inevitable bridge deal. After covering every hand except West, he showed it to the American.

Game All. Dealer South.

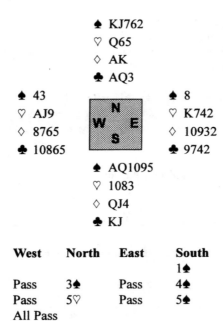

```
                      ♠ KJ762
                      ♡ Q65
                      ◇ AK
                      ♣ AQ3
    ♠ 43                              ♠ 8
    ♡ AJ9          N                  ♡ K742
    ◇ 8765      W     E               ◇ 10932
    ♣ 10865        S                  ♣ 9742
                      ♠ AQ1095
                      ♡ 1083
                      ◇ QJ4
                      ♣ KJ
```

West	North	East	South
			1♠
Pass	3♠	Pass	4♠
Pass	5♡	Pass	5♠
All Pass			

"Let me demonstrate the strengths and weaknesses of their system," he said. "I was West, playing in a team of four against an Erheim quartet. What should I lead against five spades?"

Brick studied the hand with a pronounced lack of enthusiasm. "I'm not crazy about passive leads against high level suit contracts," he hedged.

"Neither am I," Victor agreed. "So you would try a heart. I expected no less of you. But which?"

Brick took an inspirational swallow, but nothing happened. "You might explain the bidding," he suggested.

"It was most informative. North's double raise was forcing and very strong. His Five Hearts was an asking bid. South's sign-off denied first or second round control of the suit."

Suddenly Brick felt a warm glow. The cognac had reached him at the same time as the information. "Then my knave would hit the green baize at the speed of light," he announced flamboyantly.

"A brilliant choice," Victor congratulated him, and proudly revealed the other hands. "The bidding marks North with most of the high cards, and partner with the heart king. The knave caters to the actual layout. No other lead defeats the contract."

"Perhaps it wasn't so difficult to find, after that auction." Brick stubbornly refused to show how much he enjoyed the great man's praise. "But the heart holdings might be reversed, in which case you need to lead a low heart" he said.

"Possibly, but North would be reluctant to bid five hearts with three small hearts."

Brick nodded. "Of course you led the knave," he remarked with gentle irony.

"Of course. Or I would hardly have shown you the deal."

"True. What happened in the other room?"

"It was a flat board. Our team-mates were also one down."

"In five spades?"

"Six. Their auction was One Spade-Six Spades."

"*Magnifique*," Brick grinned. "But isn't it taking naturalism a little too far?" He gave his mentor a searching glance. "Tell me, Victor: why are you so dead set against conventions?"

"I'm not. I should be perfectly willing to play the Vienna system, with some modifications of my own. Stern is a genius, and a personal friend. But the Nazis have so perverted his ideas that I must oppose them with the most radical alternative. Revolutions are won by extremists, never by liberals."

Victor touched his glass to Brick's. "To our partnership," he said. "And this time I know our side will win."

"Don't get too upbeat, Victor. It's only a game of bridge."

"It is much more than that. It is a clash between two inimical cultures. It is a chance for us to…"

"Okay." Brick raised his hand in surrender. "We're here to discuss tactics, not build a world fit for heroes."

"No? Well I happen to know about your exploits in Spain and Ethiopia. You are something of a hero yourself."

"I was until I joined Daredevils Anonymous. Now I'm too yellow to swat a three-legged fly."

Victor regarded him wisely. "What do you believe in, Monsieur Lane?"

"I'm a self-made man. I believe in my creator."

"Good. I was beginning to think you regarded life as a hereditary disease."

"And the only cure is strong drink," Brick concurred. "Have another"

"You cannot drown your destiny, my friend. The Cause needs you."

"The only cause I know is Brick Lane. You overrate me, Victor. You're an idealist. You think that because a rose smells better than a cabbage, it will make better soup."

"And you are a cynic. When you smell a rose, you probably look round for a coffin. Yet you and I have more in common than you think. For example, I know you are in love with a woman. It is a sad trick of fate that I happen to love the same woman."

Brick nearly dropped his glass. "I had no idea you knew Ermintrude Butkiss!" he exclaimed.

With no visible effort, Victor managed to keep a straight face. "I ask only one thing," he said. "I cannot move in Casablanca without being followed. Even if I had a visa, I could not escape; Strafe would never permit it. But you have two letters of transit – yes, Lisa told me about them. I would like you to use them to take her to Lisbon – to America, if you wish."

"Do you love her that much?"

"Apparently you think of me only as a bridge expert. But, unlike most bridge experts, I am also a human being."

"That's something we don't have in common."

"So you have also joined Human Beings Anonymous? That is a pity, because when you go to America, I hoped you would take Ukarde's papers with you, and see that they were published."

"I see." Brick looked pensive as he sipped his cognac. "I'd like you to tell me something," he said.

"Anything."

"What do we do over their one club opening?"

Chapter Six

Everyone came to Brick's. They wanted to tell their grandchildren that they had seen the great bridge battle between the Scientists and the Naturals. Those without grandchildren came for the hell of it. The bridge refugees congregated around Victor, the expert's expert. With Lisa at his side, smiling like a Pacific sunrise, he was the class act. Fresh from the dry cleaner, his white suit seemed to symbolise the elegant simplicity of his bidding.

As the players took their seats, Brick cast a jaundiced eye over the opposition. Strafe was strictly a book man; all logic and no flair. He knew the type well: unforced errors would be as rare as virgins in Montmartre. But they were often wide open to a well-timed sucker punch.

Opposite the major sat Baron Otto von Lüdenberg, an international star, whose frigid manner and mastery of the calculated insult had ensured his rapid rise in the diplomatic service. He had mean grey eyes and thin lips, fixed in a curl of contempt for his fellow man. Brick instantly warmed to him. But the guy had the cut of a born winner. And he would not be content with victory he would have to win in style. Which might be his weak spot. Strafe won the cut for the first deal, and beamed at the kibitzers. "It appears that our friendly little game has attracted quite an audience," he said, in a voice as friendly as a castrating knife.

"The penalty of fame, Major," sighed Louis, who had placed his front row seat with exquisite neutrality, between the German and Brick.

The first deal gave Victor a chance to stamp his authority on the game.

Game All. Dealer North.

Lüdenberg
♠ QJ10
♡ 42
♢ 10842
♣ AKQ7

Brick
♠ 6543
♡ J1093
♢ K
♣ 9854

Hilo
♠ K92
♡ AQ87
♢ J95
♣ J103

Strafe
♠ A87
♡ K65
♢ AQ763
♣ 62

West	North	East	South
	1♣(i)	Pass	1NT(ii)
Pass	2NT(iii)	Pass	3♢
Pass	4♢	Pass	5♢
All Pass			

(i)   18-27 Erheim points, no long suit outside clubs
(ii) Game-forcing
(iii) 18-22, balanced

After the first three conventional bids, Strafe bid a natural three diamonds. Inwardly cursing the system, von Lüdenberg was obliged to raise, and he lifted a quizzical eyebrow when Strafe did not wheel out one of his beloved asking bids.

Brick led the ♡J to his partner's ace. Seeing Strafe's hand, Louis could confidently call the shots. Declarer would win, cross to the table and take two successful spade finesses. Then he could afford the book safety play of laying down the ◊A. When the king appeared, the defence would be history. Three no-trumps was a better contract, but Strafe's bidding blunder seemed destined to go unpunished.

But Victor hadn't read Louis' script. At trick two he switched smoothly to the ◊9. Strafe paused to consider all the combinations East could hold. Since J95 was way down the list, he finessed the ◊Q. When this lost to the king, he captured Brick's heart return and, sticking rigidly to his earlier analysis, cashed the ◊A. When Brick showed out, the major's reaction was a dazzling advertisement for the Gestapo charm school.

"Your lead of the nine of diamonds was suicidal," he ranted. "How could you know your partner did not hold the queen instead of the king? If so, I would have picked up your knave on the second round."

"No doubt," Victor agreed. "But I judged that if you held the ace-king, we had no defence."

"But why the nine?"

"Because, my dear Major, it was the card most likely to antagonise as well as deceive," Victor shrugged. "But I do not have to justify my leads to you. This is reputed to be a free country."

"And you are a freedom fighter," Strafe jeered. "I wonder why such a clever man should choose such a hopeless occupation?"

"It is in my blood," replied Victor. "My father was a freedom fighter, and so was his father before him."

"I see." Strafe leered at his ring of supporters. "And what would you have become if they had been jackasses?"

Victor thought for a moment. "Probably a Nazi," he concluded.

The roar of support from Victor's supporters was deafening. Victor stood heroically, conducting with frenetic zeal, as the room echoed to their battle cry: "*One spade, four spades, six spades, pass!*"

Strafe's men rose in a body to retaliate with their anthem: "*Erheim, Erheim, über Alles!*" A brawny SS officer strode pugnaciously towards Victor, but stopped in his tracks when Brick seized him roughly by the arm.

"I won't stand for trouble," he growled. "You can either lay off politics or get out."

The uproar died down. The spectators returned to their seats, except Louis, who had never left his. He sat, smoking urbanely, thoroughly enjoying the spectacle. Lisa, her eyes glowing, gazed lovingly at Brick, then at Victor, then back again to Brick...

"Well done, my beloved."

"Thank you, Lisa," they replied in unison.

The next deal was thrown in. Tempers cooled. Then, when the American's bold bidding kept the Germans out of a makeable game, both his opponents forgot to double. Strafe glowered as his partner dealt the next hand, while Bugatti, seated on von Lüdenberg's right, leaned confidentially towards the Baron.

"A strange customer, that Brick," he whispered.

"Really?" von Lüdenberg drawled, in a voice conspicuously devoid of interest, but intending no insult to Bugatti. As a true democrat, he believed in talking down to everybody.

"You never know what he will do next," Bugatti told him.

Brick heard this. You didn't survive in Casablanca without learning to read lips or pick up whispers. Grinning inwardly, he decided it was the ideal moment to spread a little confusion.

Game All. Dealer North.

Lüdenberg
♠ 1085
♡ QJ87
◇ KQ4
♣ 876

Brick
♠ AKQJ42
♡ 93
◇ J9
♣ AQ10

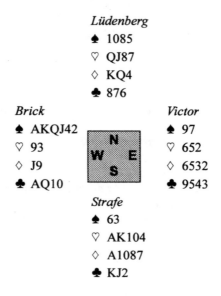

Victor
♠ 97
♡ 652
◇ 6532
♣ 9543

Strafe
♠ 63
♡ AK104
◇ A1087
♣ KJ2

West	North	East	South
	Pass	Pass	1♣(i)
Dble	Rdble(ii)	Pass	1NT(iii)
Pass!	2♣(iv)	Pass	2♡
Pass	3♡	All Pass	

(i)   18-27 Erheim points, no long suit outside clubs
(ii) 12-17 Erheim points
(iii) 24-27, balanced
(iv) Stayheim

Rick was unable to make a strong jump of Two Spades so he started off with a double. However, when the early bidding marked Victor with a blizzard, he reasoned that his best chance of a plus score was to go quietly. When his opponents subsided at the three level, he passed with what he hoped was a bored expression.

His opening lead was no problem. There was one slim chance of putting his partner in, and Brick seized it. He flicked the ♠2 nonchalantly on to the table.

What else? Strafe played low from dummy. Victor captured with his ♠7 and returned a low club. Brick placed his queen on declarer's knave, and continued with the ♠4. Suspecting nothing, Strafe again played low from the table. In with the ♠9, Victor fired back another club, to set an unbeatable contract by one trick.

Oblivious to the buzz of stunned admiration, the Baron recorded the score unemotionally, as if the defence was a routine masterpiece. Brick acknowledged Victor's salute with a faint nod; anything more would have been bad for his image. The penalty was only fifty points, but the effect on Strafe was worth a thousand.

"How can one play against such insane bidding and play?" the major almost shouted.

"Expertly," drawled von Lüdenberg.

"Then may I ask what you would have done?"

"Called for the ten of spades the second time the suit was led, It could not possibly cost and, under the admittedly bizarre circumstances, you would have made an overtrick."

This was a harsh verdict, but the Baron was not a happy man. So far he had been given no opportunity to display his skills. On the next deal, his mood turned even blacker. He seethed like a corked volcano as Victor's weak jump overcall kept him out of another game, and erupted when Strafe took an unfortunate view in defence.

"A hundred point penalty is a paltry compensation for a missed game, partner."

"But, Otto…" Strafe protested.

The Baron produced a monocle and fixed the major with the glacial stare he normally reserved for lepers with personality problems.

"Please note that I do not permit the use of my first name, except occasionally by my parents," he hissed.

This was meat and drink to the Naturals, and a body blow to the cordon of storm troopers surrounding the major. Brick looked around at the tense faces. The crowded room was turning into a powder keg. One tiny spark, and... But not yet; he hoped. He would prefer the diversion to take place a little later. Timing was everything. Meanwhile, he knew he had his opponents on the ropes.

Love All. Dealer South.

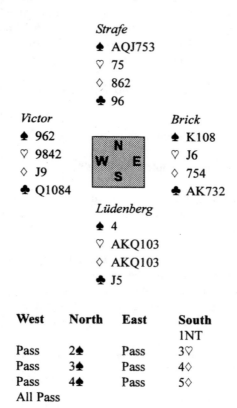

	Strafe	
	♠ AQJ753	
	♡ 75	
	◇ 862	
	♣ 96	
Victor		*Brick*
♠ 962		♠ K108
♡ 9842		♡ J6
◇ J9		◇ 754
♣ Q1084		♣ AK732
	Lüdenberg	
	♠ 4	
	♡ AKQ103	
	◇ AKQ103	
	♣ J5	

West	North	East	South
			1NT
Pass	2♠	Pass	3♡
Pass	3♠	Pass	4◇
Pass	4♠	Pass	5◇
All Pass			

After South's game-forcing 1NT opening, the Germans conducted a rare, natural auction. Victor led a small club. Brick took his two winners and switched to the ♠8. This outlandish play would have thrown most declarers, but not the Baron. He had formed a reluctant respect for Brick's defence.

Besides, he had seen situations like this before. On any other return, he could have tested trumps and, if West showed out on the second round, crossed to the ♠A to take the marked finesse. When the spade lead annoyingly deprived him of that option, his heart leapt – he knew exactly what the fellow's trump holding must be.

He favoured his opponent with a pitying smile. He seldom spoke to a member of the lower orders, but this was a special case.

"You have the distinct air of a man with four trumps to the knave," he observed, and ostentatiously finessed the ◇10.

"Baron," Brick replied evenly, "you have the distinct air of a man who has just pulled a rabbit out of an empty hat."

"I see," said the Baron, as Victor's knave appeared.

Victor was elated. Lisa glowed with approval. The refugees applauded. The storm troopers stormed. Only von Lüdenberg remained unmoved.

"I hope I have the air of a man who has just played correctly," he said.

"Oh, did you make the contract, Baron?" Strafe was determined to exact every ounce of his revenge. "May I offer my congratulations? I thought you were one down."

"My dear Major." Von Lüdenberg's tone was so contemptuous that Strafe felt as if he had been addressed as 'Corporal'. "You must learn not to equate good play with good results. But I freely acknowledge that you would have made eleven tricks."

Strafe, not at his intellectual peak, was somewhat mollified. "Thank you, Baron," he said.

"I suspect that the Baron means that it took a genius to make only ten," Victor intervened. "Well played, Baron. And, I must say, brilliantly defended, partner."

"I agree," said von Lüdenberg. "In fact, it was so brilliant that I shall include it in my forthcoming memoirs, with only one slight alteration. I shall be East," he laughed.

"Feel free," Brick said modestly. "But it wasn't difficult. On that bidding, the spade return was a standout."

"Yes," said Strafe. "I am aware of your opinion of our system."

"Oh, I heartily approve of it, Major. In future, I shall recommend it to all my opponents. Let me know when your total of conventions reaches the hundred mark. I'll bake you a cake."

So far, no contract had succeeded, and each side had one-fifty above the line. Yet the refugees were exultant: they were convinced that if Victor and the hard-bitten American had held their opponents' cards, they might well have won two rubbers.

Then Brick called time out for drinks. The others called for champagne. He called for a martini.

"Why not your usual tipple, Brick?" Louis queried.

"I missed lunch," Brick explained patiently. "I need the olive."

"For an undernourished man you are playing rather well."

"You should have seen him in Paris, Captain," said Lisa proudly.

"Yes," said Victor. "I gather that our friend was a great success in Paris, in every way. I wish I had been there."

"So does Strafe," said Louis, noticing that the major was deep in conversation with von Lüdenberg. "Would you mind keeping your voices down while I eavesdrop?"

"I disagree, Major," the Baron was saying. "I happen to be playing under two severe handicaps. One is your so-called Meistersystem..." He regarded his partner with a benevolent sneer.

"And am I to guess the other?" Strafe enquired coldly.

"I have known worse partners," the Baron conceded generously. "And if you would show more respect for the undoubted class of our opponents, you might do well enough. But they are killing us with their weak jump overcalls and pre-emptive raises. Not being able to double for penalties is like fighting a duel with an unloaded pistol."

The drinks arrived before Strafe could respond. Louis raised his glass to Brick. "To your return to the bridge scene," he proposed. "I hope it is permanent."

"My future may lie in your hands, Louis."

"Why should it?"

"You may find out at the end of the rubber."

When the Germans were ready to continue, they asked permission to exchange seats. Nobody objected, and it seemed as if the move had brought them luck. Refusing to be silenced by a daring overcall by Victor, the Baron made a treasonable leap to four spades, which he made on a textbook criss-cross squeeze.

"Do not presume to applaud," he commanded, and the awed kibitzers froze, with their hands held apart like bragging fishermen.

On the next deal, Brick made a no trump game as easily as falling off a log. The hapless Strafe had taken another wrong view in defence. Even his enemies (and he had many) would have admitted that it was a pure guess, but the supercilious expression on the face of that insufferable Baron suggested otherwise.

Strafe sorted his cards with the unmistakable air of a man who had known better evenings. He had expected to humiliate the American, to destroy his faith in that juvenile bidding system. Then the man would surely be ready to do a deal for the Stern papers. It was a classic Gestapo technique, straight from the Manual of Psychological Warfare.

But it was all going horribly wrong, Strafe knew there must be an answer, but he had no idea what it was – he had left his copy of the Manual somewhere in Berlin. He shivered. Mislaying classified documents was probably a capital offence.

He was nearly at breaking point as Victor opened one diamond.

Game All. Dealer South.

                          Brick
                          ♠ K63
                          ♡ A5
                          ◊ J65
                          ♣ AQJ87

    Strafe   *Lüdenberg*
    ♠ J109   ♠ 8742
    ♡ J9   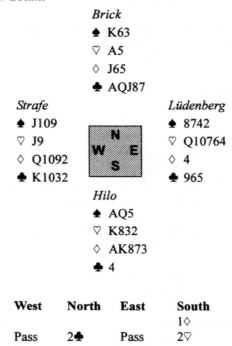   ♡ Q10764
    ◊ Q1092   ◊ 4
    ♣ K1032   ♣ 965

                          Hilo
                          ♠ AQ5
                          ♡ K832
                          ◊ AK873
                          ♣ 4

West	North	East	South
			1◊
Pass	2♣	Pass	2♡
Pass	6◊	All Pass	

For Victor and Brick, this was a marathon auction.

Strafe led the ♣J. After a great deal of thought, Victor won the lead in hand and laid down the ◊AK. Strafe, still smarting from the Baron's insult, seized the chance to impress him. He spread his hand and launched into an ill-considered explanation of Victor's error.

"You should have taken the club finesse at trick two; then you could play trumps to better advantage. After ruffing a club, you must advance a diamond towards the knave."

Victor said nothing. He gave the major a look of gentle pity, placed his cards face upwards on the table and slowly wrote down the score: plus 1370. After the merest glances, Brick and von Lüdenberg did the same.

"What are you doing?" cried Strafe. "I have two certain trump tricks."

The Baron shook his head sadly before offering his analysis: "There were several lines a competent declarer might adopt, but an immediate club finesse was not one of them. Herr Hilo's choice was the expert one: it catered for most distributions, including the present one."

"But he has two trump losers."

"So you inaccurately remarked. Now listen closely. The club ace will be followed by a club ruff. After two rounds of spades and a second ruff, a heart to the ace allows a third. The heart king is cashed, leaving the following ending with declarer on lead."

He scribbled a diagram onto the back of his scorecard. Its stark simplicity was a calculated insult.

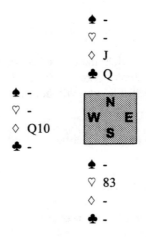

```
              ♠ -
              ♡ -
              ◇ J
              ♣ Q
♠ -         ┌─────────┐
♡ -         │    N    │
◇ Q10       │  W   E  │
♣ -         │    S    │
            └─────────┘
              ♠ -
              ♡ 83
              ◇ -
              ♣ -
```

"I trust I need not explain how declarer makes his twelfth trick. To experts, the manoeuvre is known as a *coup en passant*. Military strategists like yourself might describe it as an outflanking movement."

"But how can you be sure he would have found such a line?"

"Had there been a smidgeon of doubt, it would have vanished when you foolishly tabled your cards. But do not reproach yourself, partner; I assure you that Herr Hilo did not need any visual aids to play the hand as I would have done."

Cheering loudly, Victor's disciples rushed forward to embrace their hero. Taking no chances, the Germans formed a defensive ring around the major. This was the chance Brick had been waiting for: he leaned sympathetically towards Strafe.

"It seems like a good time for a break," he said. "Perhaps my partner and I should retire until things cool down. Shall we say half an hour?"

Chapter Seven

Brick strolled coolly into his office with Victor and Lisa. A shade too coolly, Louis thought. He lit a reflective cigarette and decided to follow them. To his surprise, Bugatti was sitting at Brick's desk as if he owned the place. When the fat man presented Brick with a fat envelope, Louis guessed that he probably did.

"Well Brick, would you like to count it?" Bugatti asked.

"I'd like to, but there's no time." Brick glanced at his watch and gave Louis his famous 'take-it-and-like-it' look. "Louis," he said, "I've sold out to Bugatti, but don't worry – he'll still let you win at roulette...if you live that long."

"Really?" Louis gave Brick his equally celebrated raised eyebrow. "Is there any reason why I shouldn't?

"I'm off to the airport – with Victor and Lisa."

"A *ménage-à-trois*. How decadent. Then I take it you have Ukarde's letters of transit?"

"You're nobody's fool, Louis. You're the only man I know who can keep both ears to the ground while he's sitting on the fence. But walking through that door was a big mistake." Brick produced a revolver and aimed it at the Frenchman's midriff. "You're coming with us to the plane. I have to be sure that you won't tip off Strafe."

"Brick, I thought we were friends."

"We are, but the gun is loaded with some very unfriendly bullets."

"Then please point it at my heart. It's my least vulnerable spot."

They hurried down to the back entrance, where Bugatti had a limousine waiting. "Farewell," he said. "I am told that there is a slight ground fog at the airport, but your plane should depart on schedule." He chuckled fatly. "I shall be intrigued to see which one of you accompanies Captain Delage on the return journey."

"I wonder what he meant?" Louis looked thoughtful as he squeezed into the car. "Of course! There are only two letters of transit. Now that is interesting."

Brick gave the gun to Victor and drove off with Louis beside him. In the back seat, Victor was curiously silent, Lisa chatted gaily about their wonderful card play, as if they were all on their way to a picnic. In ten minutes, they reached the airstrip, where the plane to Lisbon was ready to take off.

Brick stepped out onto the foggy tarmac and handed the priceless letters of transit to Louis. "You can fill in the names," he said. "That'll make them even more impressive." He paused: this was his big moment and he wasn't going to waste it. "And the names are Mr and Mrs Victor Hilo."

Lisa gasped. "But Brick," she protested. "Last night you said that you and I…"

"I said a lot of things last night," Brick muttered.

"And whatever they were, I agree with them," said Victor loftily. "You must go with Lisa. It was you who inspired her play of the knave against Dupont. It is you she truly loves."

"But you need her," Brick protested. "She's part of your work, the thing that keeps you going. Lisa, If that plane takes off without Victor, you'll regret it." His eyes were moist, probably from the fog, he told himself. "Maybe not now, but tomorrow, and for the rest of your life."

"You are wrong," Victor insisted. "I shall remain in Casablanca." He smiled winningly. This is not the time for you to be noble, partner. It doesn't go with that raincoat."

Brick fought to suppress his anger, and lost. "Then I'll do a deal with you. Get on that plane and I'll trade my raincoat for that noble white suit."

"Please stop it, both of you!" cried Lisa. She was used to men competing for her favours: the spectacle of two of them fighting to give her up was too much. Then her voice softened. "Can you not see that, in this crazy world, the problems of three little people don't amount to a deck of deuces?"

"That was poetry, Lisa," Brick's voice was thick with emotion. "I wish I'd said it."

"You will, Brick, you will." She had never looked lovelier. "Victor, you will take the Stern papers to America. And you must take Brick with you. When I watched you play together, I knew that you could become the finest partnership in the world. You must fight the Erheim system from the outside."

"But what will you do, Lisa?" Victor asked helplessly.

"I will join the bridge refugees and fight from within."

"But Lisa, you can't..." Brick and Victor began in perfect unison.

"You see?" she smiled. "You are made for each other."

There was no answer to this. Slam had been right: all men were putty in Lisa's hands. Louis wrote the names on the letters and gave them to Brick. Lisa gave Brick a chaste kiss.

"Remember, darling," she reminded him. "We'll always have Paris. And you too, Victor." She gave her husband's hand a filial squeeze. "We'll always have...wherever it was."

"Goodbye, Lisa," he said. He gave her Brick's revolver. "I shall not need this again. But you may."

As the pair trudged unwillingly towards the plane, Louis, that great opportunist, was the first to speak. "Something has just occurred to me," he said slowly. "With Ukarde out of the way, and those about to fly off, I will be the second best player in Casablanca."

"Really?" She struggled to hold back her tears. "And who will be the best?"

"Why, you will. I thought your play of the knave in Paris was masterly."

Her eyes widened. "Masterly?" she repeated incredulously.

As the engines of the plane began to purr, they heard another sound, softer, but more ominous. An open car drew up, its horn blaring. Major Strafe leapt out, and marched angrily towards them. He was alone.

"Captain!" he barked. "You have some explaining to do. Where are Hilo and Lane?"

"I am afraid they have just boarded the Lisbon plane," Louis shrugged.

"Why did you not stop them?"

Louis thought fast. "I have a superb instinct for self-preservation, Major," he said, indicating the gun in Lisa's hand. "I am told the lady is a first-class shot."

With the assurance of a born killer, Strafe drew his own pistol. "Well, she may soon discover that I am a better one." He strode to the nearby field telephone and lifted the receiver. "It is not too late to stop the plane."

"Please put down that telephone," said Lisa. She aimed, rather unconvincingly, in the general direction of his chest.

Strafe observed her with a contemptuous smirk. He had never killed a woman before, and this seemed the perfect time to start. And it would look good on his c.v. He began to squeeze the trigger, there was a loud report. He stood for a moment, his face a study in disbelief. Then, a stab of pain told him that the report had come from Lisa's gun.

That was his last thought before he died.

Louis gently confiscated Lisa's weapon. "It appears that the major is about to encounter his beloved Valkyries," he said. "You realise that this puts both of us in a very unpleasant position."

"I know, Captain."

As they watched the plane disappear into the fog, another car arrived. As it shrieked to a halt, a squad of policemen emerged, led by Lieutenant Castel. Louis' eyes swept from Strafe's corpse to Lisa, his expression unreadable.

Then he turned to his deputy.

"Major Strafe has been shot," he announced, and paused theatrically, while Lisa held her breath. "Round up the usual suspects," he commanded.

The gendarmes removed Strafe; disposing of bodies was the best part of their game. Then, with a squeal of burning tyres, they sped off, to begin their orgy of suspect-baiting.

Louis took Lisa's arm and led her towards Bugatti's limousine. "I am afraid Dupont would have made that contract had I been in your seat," he soothed her. "I should have played an uninspired ace."

"Captain," she said, "I think this could be the beginning of a beautiful partnership.

3
BRIDGE OF SPIES

Chapter One

Nick Tarrant was on the carpet. Perched nervously on the familiar hard, upright chair, he felt about as comfortable as a man making love on a row of stalagmites, with an equally sharp row of stalactites rendering movement unwise and escape unthinkable.

He considered sharing this vivid image with Control. But Control was immersed in Nick's personnel file, tut-tutting at the innumerable red flags, and glowering at his accident-prone subordinate as if he was a badly-cooked side dish he hadn't ordered.

Having digested the episode in which Nick had set back the special relationship two years by mistaking the wife of the American ambassador for an Iranian call-girl, he was staring in disbelief at the account of his latest piece of bad luck.

"Tarrant," he said, "spy-catching is at best an inexact science, and I am willing to tolerate the occasional disaster. Always provided you balance it with an occasional success." He tapped the file with an accusing forefinger. "If you have done so, it seems that your achievement has not passed into recorded history." He perused Nick's scholastic record, which made up in brevity what it lacked in quality. "I see you speak fluent Icelandic. Perhaps I should post you to Reykjavik."

Nick brightened. "Are we expecting another cod war, Sir?"

"No. Though I've no doubt you'd be quite capable of starting one."

"I'd do my best, Sir."

Control was shocked. "Tarrant, are you seriously suggesting that it is a function of this department to provoke wars?"

"I suppose not, Sir."

"I'm relieved to hear it. We only do that sort of thing when the Government is eighteen points behind in the opinion polls."

"Of course, Sir," Nick agreed fatuously.

"That was a *joke*, Tarrant." Control sighed; for a moment he seemed almost sympathetic. "But perhaps our failure to communicate is my fault. I confess I have no idea what to say to a man with a third class honours in Icelandic Studies."

"'A Big Mac and fries' is the usual ticket, Sir."

Control actually chuckled. "I like that, Tarrant. Courage under fire. For the first time in two years of consistent under-achievement, you remind me of your grandfather."

Nick blushed at the mention of the legendary Bulldog Tarrant, whose very name had struck fear into the hearts of the world's intelligence services. Especially the CIA.

"It was Bulldog Tarrant who recruited me," Control was saying. Nick recalled that his revered forebear had also recruited Kim Philby, Guy Burgess and Donald MacLean, but this didn't seem the right time to mention it.

"The Bulldog was a great man," Control continued. "And a fine bridge player. So enlighten me. How, when playing for five pounds a hundred, did you manage to lose a thousand pounds in a single day?"

"Ah!" Now that Nick knew what this interview was about, his confidence soared. "I made one slight mistake."

"And what was that?"

"I cut in at the twenty pounds game," Nick explained. "The tables weren't labelled," he added, to put the finishing touch to his defence.

"I see." Control removed a red flag, and placed it menacingly in his pending tray. "I'm relieved to hear that you didn't wantonly disobey orders. Which were…?"

"Sign in as a visitor, make a good impression, and stop playing when I'd lost fifty points." Nick grinned boyishly. "Two out of three's not bad."

"Young man, you can thank your lucky stars that we do not fire people from the Service in case they are head-hunted by a foreign power. I think that we can disregard that possibility in your case, but policy is policy."

"Thank you, Sir."

"So I will let you continue with your assignment. Stage one was to establish yourself as a desirable opponent." He frowned at Nick's expense claim. "Well you've certainly done that."

Nick's mind was racing. He had no idea why the Department was interested in a fashionable London bridge club, but from his chief's willingness to sanction the unauthorised loss of a grand, it must be something big. Or... A ghastly thought struck him. Perhaps the old sod wasn't going to pay up!

"You needn't look so worried, Tarrant. Stage two should be quite foolproof." Control gave one of his supercilious sniffs. "A necessary condition in your case."

Impervious to sarcasm, Nick leaned forward keenly as his chief continued: "Before you follow up your premature visit to the twenty pound table, we'll give you a crash course on rubber bridge. A duplicate man, aren't you?"

"A county master, Sir." Nick replied proudly.

"I see." Control looked grave. "Well it can't be helped. All of our best players are too well known to the enemy."

"The enemy?"

"That bridge game is quite possibly a medium for the passing of top secret information between two, perhaps more, of the cleverest spies of our time."

Nick stifled a gasp. In the Service, gasping was not good for the image. "Who are they?" he drawled coolly.

"Our prime suspect is a fellow named Ivan Bolkonsky. He used to be a top Russian agent. Now he's gone freelance. The end of the Cold War has a lot to answer for," he added grimly. "Did you meet the man?"

"I certainly did, Sir. He walked off with most of my money."

"The Department's money, Tarrant."

Nick felt a surge of relief. Control was going to cough up. "May I ask who the other spies are?" he asked.

"That's one of the things we need to find out." Control poured himself a cup of Earl Grey, ignoring Nick's thirsty expression. He wasn't a curmudgeonly man, but the china was Dresden. "Tell me what you made of Bolkonsky."

"Well, he didn't look like a spy, Sir."

"You amaze me. Has he stopped wearing his KGB T-shirt?"

Nick attempted a hearty laugh, but it came out as an adolescent giggle. "Anyway, he's a fantastic card player, Sir. Would you like me to show you a hand?" He took out his notebook and pen. Forty-odd years ago, Control had nearly won the Gold Cup: spectacular deals were the way to his heart.

Game All. Dealer North. N/S 60 towards.

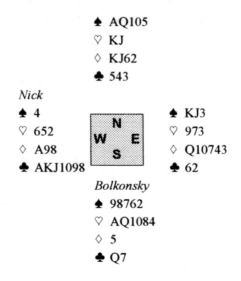

		♠ AQ105		
		♡ KJ		
		◊ KJ62		
		♣ 543		

Nick

♠ 4		♠ KJ3
♡ 652	N	♡ 973
◊ A98	W E	◊ Q10743
♣ AKJ1098	S	♣ 62

Bolkonsky

♠ 98762
♡ AQ1084
◊ 5
♣ Q7

West	North	East	South
	1NT	Pass	2♠
3♣	3♠	All Pass	

Before showing the page to his chief, Nick folded it to conceal the South and East hands. "Bolkonsky was declarer," he explained. "I began with my two top clubs. Bolkonsky dropped the queen on the second round, so I continued with the jack, and my partner discarded the *queen of diamonds*. I placed him with a singleton or doubleton, naturally."

"Why?" Control asked bleakly.

"Well, wouldn't you have done, Sir?" An odd query from a Gold Cup veteran, Nick thought. Perhaps they didn't signal doubletons in his day. "Anyway, Ivan…"

"Ivan? You've become blood brothers then?"

"Not exactly, but he started calling me Nick, and…"

"Things got out of hand. I understand, my boy. Those Ruskies aren't like us. Carry on."

"Well, Ivan ruffed and played a small diamond, all in one flowing motion. But I wasn't caught napping. In less than a minute, I rose with my ace, and when partner followed I continued the suit to give partner a ruff, Sir."

"But of course he followed suit," said Control dryly.

"Yes." Nick's eyes widened. "How did you know?"

"Because when your partner jettisoned his queen he was telling you to rise with your ace and switch, boy. Switch! I'll wager any black card would have sunk the contract." He unfolded the page to see the full deal. "I knew it," he announced triumphantly. "Your diamond continuation set the stage for a classic trump reduction."

"Thank you, Sir."

"It wasn't a compliment, you young fool. Would you like me to tell you how the play went?"

"Yes, Sir." Nick lied shamelessly.

"Bolkonsky took the trick on the table, discarding a heart from his hand. Now came three rounds of hearts. I hope you sat up when he ruffed the third round on the table?"

"I certainly did, Sir. It was a winner."

"Exactly. Guessing the situation like a true master, he cashed dummy's winning diamond, ruffed the fourth round in hand, which left:"

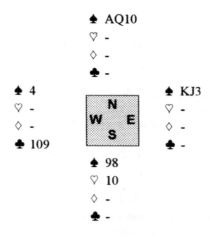

```
                    ♠  AQ10
                    ♡  -
                    ◇  -
                    ♣  -
      ♠  4                           ♠  KJ3
      ♡  -         ┌─────────┐       ♡  -
      ◇  -         │    N    │       ◇  -
      ♣  109       │  W   E  │       ♣  -
                   │    S    │
                   └─────────┘
                    ♠  98
                    ♡  10
                    ◇  -
                    ♣  -
```

"Now when your friend Ivan advanced the ten of hearts, East's goose was cooked. And you were the chef."

Nick made a desperate attempt to steer the conversation away from bridge. "May I ask a question, Sir? What sort of top secret information are they exchanging?"

"That isn't in the Need To Know category."

"But couldn't you create a Nice To Know category?"

Control pondered. "Very well," he said. "We suspect that Bolkonsky is passing vital financial information to various parties." Nick looked disappointed. "What did you expect, boy? Juicy military secrets? Why they're small beer nowadays. Finance is the coming thing. Advance warnings of changing bank rates, the latest news on our love-hate relationship with the European Exchange Rate Mechanism..." He waved a hand expansively. "That stuff is worth billions to these damned currency speculators. And you know how those blighters can play havoc with sterling."

Nick's face fell. "I'm a complete duffer at economics," he confessed.

Control seemed delighted with the news. "Really?" he beamed. "Then when this job is over, I know exactly where to post you. You're a natural for the Treasury."

Chapter Two

Mercaptan was a tall, thin academic, with a triangular face and hexagonal glasses. His receding hairline emphasised a spectacular cranial development, which caused Nick to wonder why such a mental giant should bother with anything so trivial as a card game. The man's opening remark suggested that he had read Nick's mind.

"To succeed at bridge," he declared, "you must be smart enough to play the game well, and dumb enough to believe that it matters. Control tells me that you already possess the second of those qualities."

"Kind of him," Nick seethed. "I already know you are the world's greatest cryptographer, but would you mind outlining your credentials as a bridge teacher?"

"Not at all. I played for England while I was up at Oxford, became known as the next Terence Reece, then gave up the game before it completely destroyed my sanity." He produced a rusty tobacco tin, rolled and lit a cigarette with astonishing speed, and considerately blew a cloud of smoke towards the defunct air conditioner. "I had developed a fatal allergy," he explained.

"Tobacco?" Nick asked hopefully.

"Partners." Mercaptan made the word sound like a particularly nasty virus.

"But that's what bridge is all about," Nick protested. "Everyone has partners."

"Not like mine," Mercaptan shuddered. "Mine were inflicted on me by a vengeful god. But I refused to submit to divine punishment. I fought back by reducing them to quivering jellies. Until, realising I was on the verge of graduating from verbal abuse to wilful homicide, I retired in the nick of time."

"I see," said Nick. "And does that qualify you to teach bridge?"

"Eminently. For the best advice on how to avoid sin, the chap to go to is the Devil. By the time I have finished with you, Tarrant, partners will whoop with delight when they cut you." He fixed Nick with a didactic eye. "We shall begin with the first of my commandments. And stop looking glum – none of the them forbids adultery."

They were in one of the Department's training rooms, with all the latest visual aids. Ignoring them, Mercaptan produced a crayon and wrote on the cream painted wall:

PULLING PARTNER'S PENALTY DOUBLES

1. *Don't do it*
2. *Don't even think about it*

Nick was doubtful. "I've pulled a few in my time," he said, "and got some tops."

"I believe you," Mercaptan replied dismissively. "And you've always had a travelling scoresheet to prove it. But we're discussing that irrational jungle euphemistically described as rubber bridge. Picture this: at love all, you disregard the resonant boom of your partner's penalty double, and take it out. To your intense joy, instead of setting the enemy by one paltry trick, you actually make a game. Expecting at least a grudging nod of approval from your partner, all you get is a splenetic scowl. Why? Because in the first place the donkey is convinced that they would have gone *two* down. In the second place he would rather see his putative three hundred above the line than your one-twenty below. And in the third place he can't stand having his doubles removed in the first place."

"Bad," Nick agreed.

"Bad? Let me tell you what bad is. One: Your rescue might go for a whopping penalty. Two: Your partner might have beaten them three tricks single-handed."

"But - " Nick began.

"Yes, I know exactly what you're thinking. Suppose you didn't have your previous bids? Or that you have almost no defensive values? And I must say that you expressed your doubts very lucidly. But the very poverty of your own hand might explain the stentorian quality of partner's double."

"But there must be some exceptions," Nick interpolated quickly.

"You're not ready for them yet. If you start fretting about exceptions, your body language will give crucial information to your adversaries and an ulcer to partner. Do not tax your brain with activities it is not suited for, such as thinking. Pass briskly and cheerfully."

Nick decided on a spot of mutiny. He did some thinking. "But suppose they make the contract?" he demanded.

"Splendid. You will then perform one of the most noble and profitable actions in money bridge: forgiving your partner. And with your nauseating boyish charm that should be a doddle. And now for my second commandment," he said, scribbling:

DON'T MAKE CLEVER BIDS

Nick, who had just read *Slam Bidding in the Space Age*, looked crestfallen as his mentor continued:

"Prime examples of ingenious ways to lose money are direct cue bids of the opponents' suit, and that other expensive frivolity, invitational raises to five of a major. Even experts disagree on how to respond to them, and I have known a palooka accept the invitation on the strength of an undisclosed knave in an unbid suit." Belatedly he noticed the look of hurt in his pupil's eyes. "What's the matter, Nicky? You look like a St Bernard dog who's lost his brandy. Has daddy taken away your favourite toys?"

"You'll be telling me I mustn't use Blackwood next," Nick sulked.

"Heaven forbid!" Mercaptan was profoundly shocked. "To most poor players, a slam without Blackwood is like Laurel without Hardy. Depriving them of the thrill of proving that they can count up to four is worthy of the Marquis de Sade. You haven't any sadistic tendencies, have you?"

"Not till now," Nick replied sweetly.

Loftily ignoring this feeble sally, the master returned to his theme: "Whenever you are tempted to make an arcane bid, consider these possibilities." He enumerated them with four tobacco-stained fingers. Mercaptan's ancestors had fought at Agincourt, and he had inherited both their patrician manner and their standards of personal hygiene. "One: you know what your bid means, but partner doesn't. Two: partner knows what it means but you don't. Three: neither of you knows what the hell is happening. Four: you both know what you're doing, which in rubber bridge occurs with the same frequency as a nine-card suit."

This was too much for Nick. "Surely you're exaggerating," he said.

Mercaptan considered the possibility. "You're right," he conceded. "An eight-card suit."

"Can I make SOS redoubles?" This wasn't a serious question; Nick just wanted to bait the swine. It was a waste of breath.

"Nice try, Tarrant. Just be grateful I've given you Blackwood. And now for another negative," he announced, crayon poised:

NEVER SACRIFICE

"Remember that when you write minus five hundred on your scorecard, there are no team-mates waiting to justify your bid with plus six-twenty on theirs."

"No exceptions?" Nick enquired, without much hope.

"Only one. You may sacrifice when your partner is Ivan Bolkonsky and your opponents are worse than you are. Not a likely scenario, though."

"No."

"The corollary is that if you are sitting opposite a poor player, a sacrifice only serves to prolong an unprofitable partnership."

"I see that, but…"

"Your approval fills me with hope. Once your partners regard you as sound, they will play their socks off. Mediocrity will be well within your grasp."

"Gosh!" Nick exclaimed. "You sure know how to boost a fellow's confidence."

"Irony!" Mercaptan enthused. "'Intellect on the offensive.' I was going to save my fourth commandment for another day, but now I know you possess an intellect…" He continued to deface the wall:

DON'T OVERCALL TWO OF A MINOR ON A FIVE-CARD SUIT

"Of course," Mercaptan again pre-empted his pupil, "you might hold a hand which is too strong to pass, but unsuitable for a double, or a call of one no trump. But otherwise such overcalls are just useless chatter. The odds are against your stealing the contract, and you will help your opponents more than your unfortunate partner."

This time Nick almost managed to open his mouth before Mercaptan forestalled him:

"Ah! I see that another corollary has occurred to you: you are quite right, you must be alert for opportunities to punish your opponents when they make two level overcalls. But be careful about smacking two hearts. You might double them into game."

"It isn't…"

"It isn't your money – I'd forgotten. Think of it, Tarrant: the Department is actually paying you to impersonate a bridge player."

"Yes," Nick attempted to blister the air with his response. "I have also impersonated a golfer, a gardener, a door-to-door salesman, and a rent-boy."

"I'm impressed. But they do say variety is the life of spies."

Nick had had enough. "May I say something? You are without doubt the most arrogant, opinionated, insufferable man I have ever met."

"Really?" Mercaptan was delighted. "That's the nicest thing anyone has ever said to me. I used to run a poor second to Control."

Chapter Three

After a series of gruelling tutorials, during which his initial dislike of Mercaptan blossomed into intense loathing, Nick returned to the club, confident he would survive at least half a dozen rubbers before exceeding his generously increased budget. He might even win a little. An intriguing thought struck him. Would the winnings belong to him, or the Department?

His optimism evaporated when the cut for partners pitted him against the club's two most dreaded opponents. At his left, Sir Armitage Rich, eminent banker and player of Machiavellian cunning. At his right, Bolkonsky, the man ranked by every top bridge star as the second best player in London.

The master spy looked more French than Russian; in fact he reminded Nick of Yves Montand on a bit of an off day. He wore a pearl grey suit which shrieked Saville Row, an Armani tie, and a watch designed to draw gasps of envy from people who could only afford a Rolex. As Nick dealt the cards he desperately tried not to expose his Timex.

Love All. Dealer South.

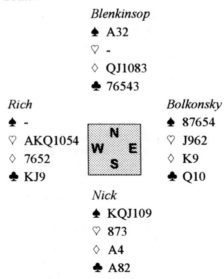

```
                    Blenkinsop
                    ♠ A32
                    ♡ -
                    ♦ QJ1083
                    ♣ 76543

    Rich                              Bolkonsky
    ♠ -               N               ♠ 87654
    ♡ AKQ1054      W     E            ♡ J962
    ♦ 7652            S               ♦ K9
    ♣ KJ9                             ♣ Q10

                    Nick
                    ♠ KQJ109
                    ♡ 873
                    ♦ A4
                    ♣ A82
```

Rich	*Blenk'sop*	*Bolkonsky*	*Nick*
West	**North**	**East**	**South**
			1♠
3♡	3♠	4♡	4♠
Pass	Pass	Dble	Redble
All Pass			

When Bolkonsky doubled his four spades, Nick redoubled like a man. The ♡A was led and the nondescript Blenkinsop put down an ideal dummy. Seeing that ten tricks were there for the taking, Nick ruffed the lead and decided to make sure of two more ruffs by spurning the diamond finesse. When at trick two he called for a low diamond, Bolkonsky played his king – an obvious singleton. Now there were twelve on top with just one more ruff – in fact thirteen looked a near certainty. Nick ruffed a heart with the ♠A and drew trumps, looking stirred but not shaken when the suit broke five-nil. This was now the position:

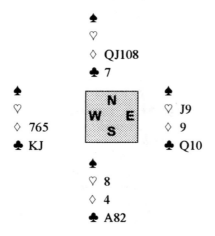

But to Nick it appeared that Rich had been dealt a 0-6-5-2 shape, probably with the ♣K9 to justify his strong jump overcall. He cashed the ♣A and gave a learned nod when the banker compounded the deception by dropping his king. Now, seduced by the dream of making three redoubled overtricks, Nick confidently finessed the ◊8, only to suffer the nightmare of a redoubled undertrick.

The Russian, a most gracious winner, especially to a valued opponent, was the first to offer his sympathy. "Bad luck, Nick," he commiserated. "But after my partner's clever play of the club king, even *I* thought I was out of diamonds."

"It's decent of you to say so."

"But I would have made the contract," Bolkonsky laughed richly. "You see, unlike you, I was brought up in a poor country. I should be grateful for two overtricks."

"Very wise," said Sir Armitage. "We capitalists are all alike. But having seen *Wall Street* nine times, I still believe that greed is good. And your dropping the king of diamonds was a superb piece of grand larceny. I was merely an accessory after the fact."

Nick regarded the banker with a thrill of interest. If Bolkonsky was receiving inside information on Britain's monetary affairs, what more likely source than a fat cat who graced the boards of at least a dozen city institutions? He cast his mind back to Control's lecture on the implications of modern surveillance techniques...

"Sir," Nick asked, "why should you suspect a bridge club?"

"Because Bolkonsky knows we're watching his every move," Control explained. "We read his mail before he does. We open every letter he posts – don't look shocked, boy, we've been doing it since 1840. We've bugged his telephone, his fax machine, his computer and every inch of his flat. Every time he breaks wind, we check in case it's in code. We follow everyone he grins at, talks to, sits next to, brushes against. If he throws away a used match, we grab it. If he dines out and leaves a dozen peas on his plate, we scrutinise them for a tell-tale pattern."

"But why a bridge club?" Nick persisted.

"My dear Tarrant, it's ideal. It is not easy for a notorious spy to hold frequent meetings with a distinguished informant without setting off all sorts of alarm bells. But he can face him daily over the green baize without causing a breath of suspicion."

"I never thought of that, Sir."

"Then it probably never occurred to you that the game is tailor made for coded messages. The way you make your bids, stack your tricks or fill in your scorecard can convey volumes. Thank God the club doesn't use bidding boxes. Why, in six auctions, Bolkonsky could translate half of War and Peace.*"*

"Then why not bug the club, Sir?"

Control was clearly embarrassed. "Gone are the halcyon days when the Service was above the law. Now we actually have to get permission." He paused, to allow the full horror to sink in. "And, as the club's membership includes two cabinet ministers and a superannuated Law Lord, it was not forthcoming. It seems, Tarrant, that the future of the nation's security rests in your hands."

Nick sat upright in his seat. "I'll bust a gut to make sure I don't let you down, Sir."

"I know you will, my boy. That's what keeps me awake at night."

Nick wrenched his thoughts back to the present. He watched the cards speeding from the plump fingers of Sir Armitage Rich. Was he telling his partner that the bank rate would fall by one per cent at noon on Wednesday? Or was he just dealing the cards?

The deal gave Nick the chance to bid and make an easy game, and he took it; reeling off winners and scorning overtricks. Then, after a competitive auction, his partner doubled Sir Armitage in an over-ambitious five diamond contract. Nick was about to take it out, but remembering Mercaptan's first commandment, he passed. Plus three hundred.

Then his luck ran out. Bolkonsky bid three slender games and made two of them. But the rubber was a close one, and Nick felt reasonably happy. He felt even happier when the same four cut again and he drew the formidable Russian.

On the first deal he made an easy two no-trump contract. Then Bolkonsky bid a poor spade slam:

Love all. North/South +70. Dealer South.

Nick

♠ QJ93
♡ KJ72
◇ A43
♣ KQ

Blenkinsop   *Rich*

```
      N
  W       E
      S
```

Bolkonsky

♠ A654
♡ A4
◇ Q865
♣ A95

West	North	East	South
			1◇
Pass	2♡	Pass	2♠
Pass	3♠	Pass	4NT
Pass	5◇	Pass	6♠
All Pass			

Nick should have responded two no-trumps; with the seventy part-score this would have been a mild slam try, which his partner would have passed.

The ♣10 was led. Bolkonsky ran the ♠Q, on which Rich played the eight and Blenkinsop the seven. The master spy thought for two tense seconds. The opening lead appeared to be from shortage, so he called for a small spade from the table and smiled when the banker produced the ♠K. He drew the last trump, cashed a second club and played three rounds of hearts, ruffing the third. If the ♡Q dropped he was home. It didn't; West discarded a diamond. The club ace came next, on which West discarded another diamond.

At this point Bolkonsky gently tabled his cards: "I'll give you a diamond."

"If it's all the same to you, I'd prefer two," said Blenkinsop tartly.

"My friend, you were dealt three spades, two hearts and two clubs. Since your remaining cards are all diamonds I shall play a low one from both hands, and I'm afraid you must lead away from your king. Bad luck."

This was the full deal:

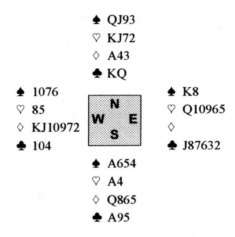

```
                    ♠ QJ93
                    ♡ KJ72
                    ◇ A43
                    ♣ KQ
      ♠ 1076                      ♠ K8
      ♡ 85           N            ♡ Q10965
      ◇ KJ10972   W     E         ◇
      ♣ 104          S            ♣ J87632
                    ♠ A654
                    ♡ A4
                    ◇ Q865
                    ♣ A95
```

Nick gazed at his country's enemy with a degree of admiration which might well have been treasonable. "That was absolutely brilliant," he gushed.

"You are much too kind. I owe it all to the great Soviet education system, which taught me to count up to thirteen. We couldn't afford calculators."

The rubber continued scrappily. Blenkinsop, ignoring his partner's repeated sign-offs, bid a slam, which, requiring adequate dummy play, went one off. Several contracts failed when trumps broke fiendishly. Nick relished every minute, watching the way Sir Armitage stacked his tricks, recorded the score and sipped his whiskey. Bolkonsky was calm, relaxed and seemingly oblivious to the banker's actions. But Nick wasn't fooled for a moment; he knew that the agent possessed two of the essential attributes of the master spy: phenomenal peripheral vision and an eidetic memory.

"Why don't you go back to Moscow?" Sir Armitage asked ruefully, when a clever false card had defeated his cast-iron contract.

Bolkonsky explained. "It appears that Communism is on its way back. It is a race which everyone wins, but nobody gets a prize."

"Now, now, Ivan, you mustn't wash your dirty Lenin in public."

Nick screwed up his face in an effort to memorise this. It sounded like a joke, but Mercaptan might decipher it as a covert message to sell sterling.

The next deal provided a keen battle of wits between the two conspirators:

North/South Game. Dealer North.

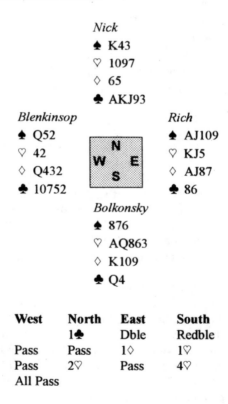

Nick
- ♠ K43
- ♡ 1097
- ◇ 65
- ♣ AKJ93

Blenkinsop
- ♠ Q52
- ♡ 42
- ◇ Q432
- ♣ 10752

Rich
- ♠ AJ109
- ♡ KJ5
- ◇ AJ87
- ♣ 86

Bolkonsky
- ♠ 876
- ♡ AQ863
- ◇ K109
- ♣ Q4

West	North	East	South
	1♣	Dble	Redble
Pass	Pass	1◇	1♡
Pass	2♡	Pass	4♡
All Pass			

When Blenkinsop led the ◇2, his eminent partner did some rapid thinking. If the lead were from the king, there was no room for West to have another high card, and declarer would lose only two diamonds and a heart. So, as the ♣Q would be waste paper, the banker had to assume that partner held a major-suit honour. If it was the ♡Q, the contract was doomed anyway, but what if it was the ♠Q? Now, if Sir Armitage took his ◊A, there would be no entry to partner's hand, and no killing lead through dummy's ♠K. The lucky Russian would be able to ruff a diamond, pick up East's trumps and discard his spades on dummy's clubs.

Pleased with his analysis, the banker played a masterly ◊J. Without hesitation, Bolkonsky produced his counter-stroke: he ducked, severing the defense's communications. When Sir Armitage continued with two more rounds of diamonds, the second was ruffed on the table with the ♡10. The ♡9 was led and Sir Armitage smartly produced the ♡K. Bolkonsky captured with the ace, overtook the ♣Q in dummy and took another heart finesse. After drawing the outstanding trump, he calmly finessed the ♣9, and was now able to claim.

Nick's mathematical ability was just sufficient for him to calculate that the rubber had netted him five or six hundred pounds. "Thank you, partner," he said with fervour.

"As well you might," said the banker. "Can I blame my defeat on your Soviet education, Ivan? Or were you born a genius?"

Bolkonsky considered the question. "As my schools shamefully neglected the art of dummy play, I must reluctantly support the second of those options," he replied.

Chapter Four

Control nodded sagely when Nick confided his suspicions about Sir Armitage Rich. "I think we may be on to something, Tarrant. The fellow always was an unmitigated bounder," he said. "He used to fag for me at school."

"I wasn't aware of that, Sir."

"*He* was." Control said with sadistic glee. "Painfully."

Nick blessed the fact that he had received his education in the post-flogging era. Although if Control and Mercaptan had been *his* fags...

"It's a pity we no longer send traitors to the Tower," Control was saying.

"But I'll put a team upon him straight away. Have you any leads on the third member of the chain?"

"What chain, Sir?"

"Good grief! Don't you remember what they taught you at basic training school?"

"It must have been the week I had measles, Sir."

"Measles? Didn't you have them as a child?"

"Yes, Sir. Twice."

"It's a wonder you're still alive." He moved his chair further away from Nick. "A man like Bolkonsky works like a pickpocket. As soon as he lifts a wallet, he passes it to an accomplice. That way he can never be caught with the goods."

To Nick this seemed unnecessarily convoluted, but he supposed top spies tended to become obsessed with their own ingenuity. But it wouldn't do to say so; in his heyday the old boy may have been a top spy himself. "I'll keep my eyes open, Sir."

"Do that. In the meantime, have you any good hands for me?"

Nick described Ivan's three brilliancies, presenting each deal as a single dummy problem. In every case, Control unerringly found the line chosen by the Russian. What a player he must have been in his prime.

◇ ◇ ◇ ◇ ◇

As Myra Bellingham gazed lovingly at her hand, Nick gazed lovingly at Myra Bellingham.

For the fourth time Myra was between husbands. Her first, Jack Bellingham, was a middle-aged arms dealer, whose fatal heart attack had occurred during a high-spot of their honeymoon. The undertaker swore that the smile on Jack's face was wider than the coffin. After each of her subsequent divorces, she reverted to his surname in honour of his memory and her achievement.

Nick had always been drawn to older women, especially when, like Myra, they had gone prematurely blonde. Her face and figure were a triumph of nature, twice-weekly beauty treatments, and state-of-the-art cosmetic surgery. Some might say that she wore too much make-up and too little clothing, but not Nick. He leaned back in the kibitzer's seat and surrendered to true love.

Myra had no intention of steering all the contracts into the Russian's hands. She paid handsomely for her pleasures, and putting down the dummy was not one of them.

Love All. Dealer South.

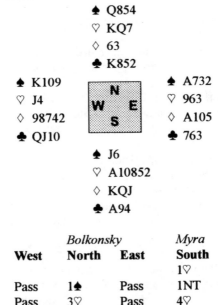

```
              ♠ Q854
              ♡ KQ7
              ◊ 63
              ♣ K852
   ♠ K109                  ♠ A732
   ♡ J4         N          ♡ 963
   ◊ 98742    W   E        ◊ A105
   ♣ QJ10       S          ♣ 763
              ♠ J6
              ♡ A10852
              ◊ KQJ
              ♣ A94
```

	Bolkonsky		*Myra*
West	**North**	**East**	**South**
			1♡
Pass	1♠	Pass	1NT
Pass	3♡	Pass	4♡
All Pass			

The ♣Q was led. Myra thanked her partner in a seductive contralto voice which sent icy fingers running down Nick's spine. It was black magic. It was a no-hope contract. There seemed no realistic chance of disposing of a club loser. Declarer might play on spades, praying for a favourable lie and a defensive error. But one look at Myra's stolid looking opponents told Nick that they lacked the imagination to make a mistake of such magnitude. The woman he adored was in trouble up to her three-tier pearl necklace, and he was powerless to help her.

But Myra had no need of a knight errant. She gave the club queen a look of mild interest and coolly played low from both hands. When West doggedly continued the suit, she won in hand, drew trumps and threw a spade loser on the fourth club.

Bolkonsky gazed at her with open admiration. "Absolutely breathtaking," he said.

"Thanks, Ivan, darling," Myra replied coquettishly. "But what did you think of my dummy play?"

"It was deliciously wicked," he laughed. "Don't you think so, Nick?"

"Rather," Nick agreed. "I shouldn't have had the nerve to duck. I suppose I would have played on spades and hoped for a miracle."

"I considered it, darling, but I'd never before ducked with four top losers. And whenever I'm faced with two evils, I always choose the one I've never tried before."

Their eyes met. Nick's heart was pounded so fiercely he was afraid it might be audible. Impossible, he decided; that sort of thing only happened in Edgar Allen Poe. He regarded his suspect dispassionately. Anyone capable of such risqué remarks and audacious play was a potential menace to queen and country. As the rubber progressed, he studied the way she watched Bolkonsky's every move.

On the next deal, after some shameless overbidding by his beautiful partner, Ivan had to play well to get out for one down in a small slam. His eleven tricks were placed at widely varying angles. Surreptitiously, Nick made a note of the pattern.

"Sorry, partner," Myra cooed. "Did I overcook it?"

"Overcook it?" Ivan replied cheerfully. "My dear Myra, it was like one of King Alfred's cakes, but I took it as a compliment to my card play." He turned suddenly to Nick. "If you are going to record my hands, Nick, please confine your efforts to my successes. Imagine that I am Doctor Johnson, and you are the fawning Boswell."

The rest of the evening was sheer bliss. Bolkonsky had to leave early, and Nick partnered Myra in three winning rubbers. When the other players had gone home, Nick gave her a shy smile.

"Playing with you has been one of my most wonderful experiences," he gushed.

"Thank you, darling." The look she gave him made his knees melt. "You don't look as if you've had all that many."

"I'm afraid you're right."

"Don't be afraid, Nick. I've always found inexperience an irresistible quality."

"Well, I've got a lot of it," he said. "I say, would you mind awfully if I invited you to supper?"

"Not if it's somewhere expensive," she replied. "Then, if you go on saying charming things to me, we can crack open a bottle of champagne … at my place."

He took a deep breath. "Where would you like me to take you?" he asked.

"Oysters are in season," she said.

"So they are," he said, trying to sound sophisticated.

"They are supposed to be an aphrodisiac," she smiled. "We'll have a dozen each and see how many of them work."

Control wore a judicial frown as he considered Nick's description of Myra's coup. "I concede that it was a shrewd gamble," he said. "But I'm surprised Bolkonsky made such a fuss about it. Ducking the club lead is automatic to a player of his class. You saw how I spotted the line in a flash."

"You always do, Sir."

"Thank you, Tarrant. It seems that my old skills haven't entirely deserted me.

And in return, I congratulate you on your perceptive analysis of Mrs Bellingham. She may well be the final link in the chain."

"But she may also be an unwitting accomplice, Sir. Even if she is passing coded messages from Bolkonsky to another party, she might not know what they mean. Bolkonsky may be like you, Sir, operating on the Need To Know basis, in which case Myra – I mean Mrs Bellingham – isn't a spy, technically speaking, that is."

"I see," Control's supercilious sniff was accompanied by an equally unpleasant smirk. "Attractive lady, is she?"

"Yes, Sir. I suppose so…fairly."

"You surprise me. But never let blonde hair and a pair of big blue eyes cloud your judgement. Remember Mata Hari."

"She was a bit before my time, Sir."

"I'll have you know she was a bit before *my* time. But her story is a lesson to us all. So keep a close eye on Mrs Bellingham."

"I've already started, Sir." Nick's hand crept gingerly towards the extortionate restaurant bill in his inside pocket. "Last night I put in a spell of overtime."

"There is no such thing as overtime in the Service. Next thing you'll be telling me you took her to supper at the Department's expense. Treasury would go berserk."

"Of course, Sir." Nick sighed and returned an empty hand to his lap. Control watched him with a malicious smile. "I hope she was worth it, my boy." He stood up and rubbed his hands in anticipation. "Now, have you any good deals for me?"

"Even better, Sir. I have diagrams of how Bolkonsky stacks his tricks."

"Pop them along to Mercaptan, that's his speciality. Mine is high level card play."

Stung by his chief's refusal to sanction his lavish outing, Nick had a childish urge to pretend there were no hands worth mentioning. Then he noticed the equally childish look of expectation on the ageing face, and relented. After recounting two minor masterpieces, he proudly displayed his star deal:

North/South Game. Dealer West.

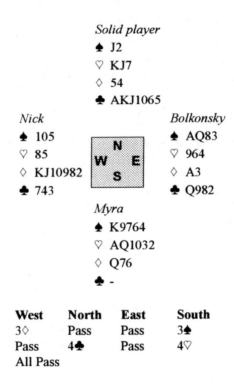

Solid player
♠ J2
♡ KJ7
♢ 54
♣ AKJ1065

Nick
♠ 105
♡ 85
♢ KJ10982
♣ 743

Bolkonsky
♠ AQ83
♡ 964
♢ A3
♣ Q982

Myra
♠ K9764
♡ AQ1032
♢ Q76
♣ -

West	North	East	South
3♢	Pass	Pass	3♠
Pass	4♣	Pass	4♡
All Pass			

"A very poor contract," Control observed.

"Yes, Sir. Myra gets into a lot of those. We began with three rounds of diamonds. She ruffed the third with dummy's jack, and played a spade towards the king. Her luck was in when it held, but there was still a lot of work to do. She played a spade to the jack: Ivan captured this with the ace, and -"

"Let me jot down the position," Control interrupted eagerly.

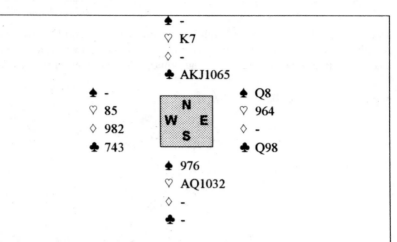

"That's right, Sir. And Ivan led a trump."

"Not *a* trump, Tarrant. The *nine*! It gave declarer no better option than to win in hand, and ruff a spade with dummy's last trump, the king, while you threw a club. Now she was able to discard her last two spades on dummy's top clubs, but observe."

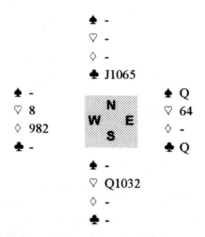

"Because of your heart eight, she had to ruff high, promoting Bolkonsky's six."

"I know, Sir. I was there."

"But what would have happened if your partner had led a low heart at trick six? Declarer would let it run to dummy, covering whichever card you played. Now she cashes two top clubs, discarding spades. Then it's plain sailing; a club-spade cross ruff, and because she has been allowed to retain her three honours, *no trump promotion*." He looked smug. "But it wasn't to be, thanks to fine defence."

"Thank you, Sir."

"Not you, you young fool – Bolkonsky. And I was with him every step of the way. Our lead of the trump nine was masterly."

"You certainly work well together, Sir," Nick murmured.

Control was too busy preening himself to hear him. "I trust the day will never dawn when I can't match anything a KGB man can do."

"Ex-KGB man," Nick corrected him gently.

"Exactly, Tarrant. We've had a few Mexican stand-offs in the past, but that was when he could command ten times my resources. But now..." He broke off, as if he wanted to enjoy his fantasy in silence.

Nick stared at him in mute incredulity. This was a side of Control he had never seen. The man actually seemed human. And it was not a pleasant sight.

Chapter Five

"I can recommend the pressed boar's head," said Ivan, as he tasted his Imperial Tokay.

After sampling his sinful peach brandy cocktail, Nick was feeling reckless. "I'll try anything once," he said.

"Then leave everything to me." The Russian instructed the waiter in fluent Hungarian, and regarded his guest with fatherly affection. They were enjoying a late supper in a Magyar restaurant, where two could dine well for the price of a redoubled overtrick. "I am delighted you have joined the club, Nick."

"Of course you are, Ivan. I must be your main source of income."

"You're too modest. Do you realise that we have won about three thousand pounds on partnership?"

"Probably because I let you play all the contracts."

Bolkonsky lifted his glass in a charming salute, and poured Nick a generous measure of Tokay. "Your bidding is sound; it has the unmistakable stamp of Mercaptan. I imagine your losses are well within your department's budget."

Nick nearly choked on his wine. "Budget?" he spluttered. "What budget?"

"My dear young friend, I too was the slave of a soulless bureaucracy. When those grey men at the top of the pyramid sift through their paperwork, the only bits they truly understand are our expense claims, which they peruse with the fervour of a dowager duchess vetting a prospective son-in-law. Take Control. As long as he justifies his request with a hundred-page report, he will be granted an extra surveillance team without question. But if one of the team has to follow his quarry into the Savoy, he will have a hard time justifying two cups of coffee."

Bolkonsky was a kindly man. He had spoken at length to allow his guest to recover from the shock. But all Nick could do was goggle like a startled goldfish and wonder why his training hadn't included what to do when the chap you are spying on takes you to supper to tell you that you have blown your cover to smithereens. He downed his Tokay in a single gulp. Bolkonsky gave him a medicinal refill.

"Your illustrious surname was the first clue. Bulldog Tarrant was before my time, but the KGB worshipped him. He recruited so many closet communists that we nearly made him a Hero of the Soviet Union."

Nick managed a sickly grin. "What were the other clues?"

The waiter arrived with their starters, and Bolkonsky sent him off for some more Tokay. "To begin with," he said, "I was painfully aware of some heavy-handed surveillance. It was only a matter of time before it reached my bridge club. They didn't follow us here, though," he added reassuringly.

Nick recollected their breakneck journey from the club. A car had drawn up, as if by prior arrangement. Having named a destination in Chelsea, Bolkonsky changed his mind after half a mile, and the grinning driver executed a hair-raising U-turn to begin a nightmare trip to Soho. Ignoring such irrelevancies as red lights and no-entry signs, he weaved recklessly through a maze of side streets to a dark alley near the restaurant. So much for Control's faith in modern surveillance techniques!

"Clue number two, Nick, you must learn to temper your curiosity with subtlety. But I must commend the zeal with which you ogled my every move. Also the horseradish sauce; it goes superbly with boar's head."

Amazingly, Nick discovered that he had a ravenous appetite. He tucked in with gusto, as the Russian resumed his lesson.

"When your eagle eye alighted on Armitage Rich, I guessed you had him down as my informant. But it was when you focussed on the delectable Myra Bellingham that I knew you had been reading too much John le Carré. I gather she took you back to her flat the other evening. I trust you remembered to lay back and think of England."

They were in an alcove, secluded from the main dining area, and Nick prayed that his crimson cheeks wouldn't show in the dim light, or that Ivan would attribute them to the horseradish. But how dare the man mistake his pure romantic love for carnal desire! Even if four of the oysters *had* worked.

Bolkonsky was laughing, but not at Nick. "Admit it," he said. "Control actually believes I am peddling financial information. Doesn't he realise that with the Cabinet leaking government policies like a colander, state secrets have the market value of last year's bananas?"

"But Control said…"

"Control, my friend, has a single ruling passion: to rescue his department from the jaws of obsolescence. With no more communists under every bed, he has to invent a new set of bogeymen. The poor fellow is senile."

Nick leapt to the defence of his chief. "He's still a jolly fine bridge player. I've shown him all your triumphs, and he always finds your winning line."

Bolkonsky frowned. "Now that surprises me." Nick was lost in admiration as the Russian jotted down every card of a deal played several days ago. "I take it you told the chief about this one?" said Bolkonsky. "Did you emphasise my desperate, but ill-fated defence to a well-played four spades?"

Love All. Dealer East.

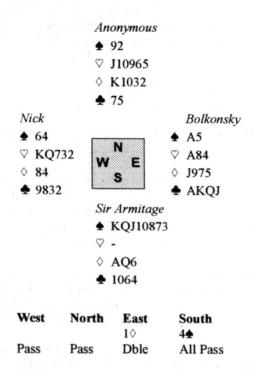

Anonymous
♠ 92
♡ J10965
◇ K1032
♣ 75

Nick
♠ 64
♡ KQ732
◇ 84
♣ 9832

Bolkonsky
♠ A5
♡ A84
◇ J975
♣ AKQJ

Sir Armitage
♠ KQJ10873
♡ -
◇ AQ6
♣ 1064

West	North	East	South
		1◇	4♠
Pass	Pass	Dble	All Pass

"Of course I emphasised it," said Nick. "I always emphasise your brilliancies."

"Your faith is touching," Bolkonsky smiled. "But I'm afraid it is about to be severely tested. Let's see if you can recall the play, which you admire so much."

"I think so," said Nick hopefully. "I led the eight of diamonds. Sir Armitage won with his ace, and played the king of spades. You took the trick and cashed one top club. I signalled with the eight and you now exited with your remaining trump." He paused. "You'd better take over."

"By all means. Rich cashed the diamond queen and ran his trumps. Anticipating an end-play, I started to unblock clubs. This was the position when the last trump was led:"

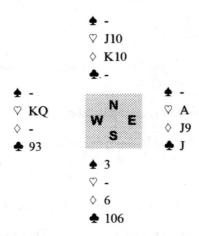

```
                    ♠ -
                    ♡ J10
                    ◊ K10
                    ♣ -
    ♠ -                          ♠ -
    ♡ KQ          N              ♡ A
    ◊ -        W     E           ◊ J9
    ♣ 93          S              ♣ J
                    ♠ 3
                    ♡ -
                    ◊ 6
                    ♣ 106
```

"I remember," said Nick, excitedly. "Your only hope was to find me with the club ten, so you jettisoned your knave. When Sir Armitage produced the ten, he said 'Bad luck, Ivan', which I thought was jolly sporting of him."

"I am more interested in what Control said when you showed him the hand."

"He was his usual brilliant self, Ivan. He defended just as you did, card for card."

"Then he played as crassly as I did. He should have ducked the first round of trumps. Now if declarer plays a second, East will simply cash two more rounds of clubs."

"Of course!" Nick slapped his forehead with the palm of his hand while Bolkonsky asked the waiter to hold back the main course and bring two large vodkas.

"You didn't mention your mistake at the time," said Nick.

"I should think not. My reputation for infallibility is worth thousands a year. But inwardly I cursed my idiotic lapse. On a difficulty scale of one to ten, the hand rates a three at most. Yet the man who nearly won the Gold Cup chose the same fatuous line as I had. Now think carefully, Nick. When you told him about my defence to Myra's four hearts, did he find the lead of the nine as quickly as I did?" Nick nodded reluctantly. "I thought as much. And with all due modesty, I would give my trump promotion a difficulty rating of at least eight."

"Ivan, what are you suggesting?"

"It's obvious. He has the club bugged. He has all my coups on film, and reproduces them... *uncritically*."

"Then why does he waste time asking me about them?"

"It makes you feel useful, and it allows him to show you what a great player he is. You should see the KGB's psychological profile on Control. On a vanity scale of nought to ten, he scores eleven point five."

"But he told me he couldn't get permission to bug the club."

"And you believed it. Dammit, until ten minutes ago, *I* believed it! When you arrived on the scene, dripping clues like an Agatha Christie novel, it never occurred to me to suspect hidden cameras as well. I am sorry, Nick, but you are nothing more than a decoy. And all the more convincing because you don't realise it."

The vodkas arrived. The Smirnoff ads were right; the stuff certainly made you see things differently. Nick recalled Control's inspired guesses; that Myra was a blonde; that Nick had taken her to an expensive supper; the strange lack of interest in his diagrams of Ivan's card patterns – easily explained if they already had them on film.

"I still don't believe it," he said.

"Have some more vodka, and you may find that you do."

Nick took the Russian's advice. It worked. "I shall resign," he said.

"Why? Think of what you'll be giving up; an élite bridge education, at Control's expense; suppers like this, at my expense; the buxom Myra..." He leaned forward persuasively. "And with a little help from your friends, you can really milk the situation. If we feed Control the occasional titbit, you can enjoy the good life indefinitely."

As he spoke, Bolkonsky had considerately switched his full glass of vodka for Nick's empty one. The act seemed to symbolise something, but Nick wasn't sure what. "Are you asking me to become a double agent?" he demanded, in his best red, white and blue voice.

"Of course not. But occasionally the interests of your country and mine coincide." He produced a photograph. "Do you recognise this man?"

Nick found himself staring at the likeness of a man in his mid-forties, dark, tough and definitely not nice to know. He shook his head.

Bolkonsky returned the photograph to his note-case. "His name is Denisov. Ex-KGB. He was no great loss; his bidding was execrable."

"Where is he now?" Nick asked, for no particular reason.

"If my information is correct, he is dining in the main body of the restaurant. I don't want him to see me, so I would like you to go to the cloakroom and see if he has arrived. Discreetly, please."

Without knowing why, Nick obeyed the Russian's instructions. Denisov was busily eating pressed boar's head, evidently the in-dish for master spies. He returned to the table. "Your man is there, Ivan."

"Ugly brute, isn't he? He is now with the Russian Mafia. Next Thursday, he will be handing over a large consignment of drugs to his British customer."

"And what do you want me to do? Surely it's a job for the police."

"I know, Nick, but I suggest you inform Control. He'll pass it to Special Branch, but he will get the credit, and you will become his blue-eyed boy."

"Sounds good." Nick sipped his vodka. "And what do you get out of it, Ivan?"

"I still do the odd job for the KGB. My contacts want to get rid of Denisov, but not on their own doorstep. He has powerful friends."

"So why don't you tip off Special Branch direct?"

"Because we couldn't trust them not to reveal their source. Nick, there is only one man in the business whom we really trust. And he is sitting at my table."

Nick stifled the urge to look round to see who had joined them. "That is a very nice compliment, Ivan," he said hoarsely.

"I am sure you will live up to it, my friend. But Control must never know that the tip came from me. Tell him we came here for supper, and I bumped into an old acquaintance. He looked a shady character, so when he went to make a call from the telephone next to the toilet, you followed him. I shall give you a transcript of what you will claim to have overheard, and we will rehearse it till you are word perfect."

The vodka had raised Nick's powers of perception to a new high point. He searched Ivan's plan for flaws. And found one.

"Ivan," he said. "Before I agree, can you promise me one thing?"

"What is it, Nick?"

"That this time, I'm not just a decoy."

Chapter Six

On the morning of the following Friday, Nick was in Control's office, lounging in a comfortable armchair, and sipping Earl Grey tea from a Dresden cup.

"Would you care for a biscuit, Tarrant?"

"No, thank you, Sir," said Nick, in the tone of a man who was living too well to need snacks between meals.

Control gave him a beam of approval which must have put tremendous strain on the unused muscles of his face. "A good show all round, Tarrant," he said, in the tone of a man whose department has been granted a new lease of life. "Yesterday evening, after some brief armed resistance, we nabbed the whole gang red-handed. The only casualty was the chap you spotted, name of Denisov. Bullet through the heart. We've no idea who fired it."

"Very odd, Sir."

"Tell me, do you think Bolkonsky could have been involved in the business?"

"I doubt it, Sir. I'm sure the meeting in the restaurant was a complete coincidence."

"Then how do you account for the way he shook off our surveillance team by that death-defying U-turn?"

"Another coincidence, Sir. We were going for Chinese. It was I who suggested Hungarian. And those Ruskies aren't like us, Sir. They're always acting on impulse."

"True." Control took a reflective sip. He gazed out of the window, with his back to Nick. "I suppose it's too much to hope for another fortuitious encounter with a Russian super-criminal?"

If Nick had been sitting on Control's punishment stool, he would have fallen off. Had the old man seen through the scam? Or was he just sighing for the moon? "I shouldn't think so, Sir," he said. Then he had an inspiration. "But there have been so many lucky coincidences that I wouldn't bet against another one. Perhaps I should take Ivan to a few of his favourite restaurants."

"Make it so. By the way, Mercaptan says he's well on the way to cracking Bolkonsky's trick-stacking code. You'd better step up your activities in the club…which reminds me. If you still have the tab for that feast with your merry widow, I think I might be able to swing it with the people on the top floor."

"That's very good of you, Sir." Nick deftly produced the restaurant bill and placed it meaningfully in Control's Immediate Action tray. "Shall I continue to keep an eye on her, Sir?"

"A good idea, my boy." Control's eyes bulged as they alighted on the bottom line of the bill, but he made a Herculean recovery. "After all, I'm told that consignment we confiscated had a street value of fifty million."

"Does that mean we're going into the drugs market, Sir?"

"Very good, er…Nick." Control's chuckle made up for in deference what it lacked in sincerity. Nick decided to ride his luck. He peered ostentatiously into his empty cup.

His host's response staggered him. He rose, and took Nick's cup to the teapot. It was received wisdom that the only visitor Control ever waited upon was the Home Secretary. He decided it was the perfect moment to go for gold. Lesser men would have asked for promotion, a medal or an official car.

But not Nick.

"Sir," he said. "I appreciate your calling me Nick, but I wonder if ... when we're alone ... you could see your way to making it ... Bulldog?"